The Poems of

# John Dewey

Edited
with an Introduction by
## Jo Ann Boydston

Southern Illinois University Press
Carbondale and Edwardsville

*Feffer & Simons, Inc.*
London and Amsterdam

CENTER FOR EDITIONS OF
AMERICAN AUTHORS
*AN APPROVED TEXT*
MODERN LANGUAGE
ASSOCIATION OF AMERICA
®

This edition of *The Poems of John Dewey* had as its associate textual editors Barbara Levine and Lynn Ziegler, of the Center for Dewey Studies, Southern Illinois University at Carbondale.

John Dewey's poems are published with the permission of the John Dewey Foundation. Anzia Yezierska's works are quoted with the permission of Louise Levitas Henriksen.

Copyright © 1977 by Southern Illinois University Press
All rights reserved
Printed in the United States of America
Designed by Gary Gore

Library of Congress Cataloging in Publication Data

Dewey, John, 1859–1952.
  The poems of John Dewey.

  Includes indexes.
  1. Boydston, Jo Ann, 1924-
PS3507.E878P6   1977        811'.5'4        77-4718
ISBN 0-8093-0800-2

Tho all the rhymes were long since rhymed
And in by-gone ages songs were all sung,
There are heights of joy not yet climbed,
And hearts not yet by sorrows wrung.

Like to bodies of babes new born
My lines repeat what's old and worn;
Yet both may bear beneath their shells
Fresh joys, and woes of fresh made hells.

—John Dewey

# Chronology of the Deweys, 1904–1929

1904    John and Alice resign from University of Chicago in April.

1904    Family goes to Europe in June, joined by Dewey later in summer.

1904    Death of Gordon in Ireland in September.

1905    Dewey begins his professorship at Columbia University in February; family remains in Europe, where he joins them in June.

1909    Family buys farm at Huntington, L. I.

1913    Alice and Evelyn go to Switzerland where Lucy and Jane are in school, then to Italy to spend winter. John, Lucy, and Jane join them in April 1914.

1917–18    From October to May, Anzia Yezierska attends Dewey's seminar in Social and Political Philosophy.

1918    Dewey gives "Human Nature and Conduct" lectures at Stanford University in May; he and Alice take an apartment in San Francisco.

1918    John, Evelyn, and Lucy spend the summer at the farm; Dewey commutes to Philadelphia for Polish study; Alice and Jane remain in San Francisco.

1918–19    Dewey has sabbatical leave this academic year.

1919    Alice and John go to Tokyo; Dewey lectures at the Imperial University.

1919–21    Lucy and Evelyn join their parents in China; Dewey lectures at National University of Peking, National Teachers Colleges of Peking and Nanking.

1921    Family returns to United States in October.

1924    Dewey serves as educational consultant to Turkish government in summer. Alice becomes seriously ill in September.

1925    Huntington farm is sold in November.

1926    Dewey is visiting professor at the University of Mexico in the summer. Alice returns early because of illness.

1927    Dewey takes leave from Columbia spring semester to take care of Alice.

1927    Death of Alice in July.

1928    Dewey makes educational survey in Russia.

1929    Dewey gives Gifford Lectures at University of Edinburgh in April and May.

1929    Celebration in October of Dewey's seventieth birthday.

# Contents

|   | Introduction | ix |
|---|---|---|
| 1 | Lyric Poems | 1 |
| 2 | Nature Poems | 33 |
| 3 | Philosophical Poems | 45 |
| 4 | Children's Poems | 69 |
| 5 | Appendix Poems | 75 |
|   | Description of the Texts | 81 |
|   | Editorial Method | 93 |
|   | Regularization Lists | 97 |
|   | Apparatus for Poems | 99 |
|   | Index of Titles | 148 |
|   | Index of First Lines | 151 |

# *Introduction*

MORE than ninety typed and handwritten poems found in John Dewey's desk and wastebasket—and assumed to be his compositions—were in the Columbiana Collection at Columbia University in the care of the Curator, Milton Halsey Thomas, for a number of years after 1939 when most of them were discovered. In 1957, five years after Dewey's death, a scholar from France, Gérard Deledalle, saw the poetry among other Dewey materials in Columbiana, copied it out, and asked Dewey's widow—his second wife, Roberta—for permission to edit and publish it. Up to that time, Mrs. Dewey had not known about the existence of the poetry or the large body of other Dewey material in the Columbiana Collection; but, upon learning of the twenty-plus boxes Thomas had collected over the years, including the poetry, she asserted her legal right to the Dewey materials and persuaded the University to relinquish them.

Within a year after she gained possession of the poetry, Roberta Dewey took steps toward having it published; she asked Charles A. Madison, Dewey's former editor at Henry Holt and Company, to look at the poems and to inquire whether Holt would be interested in publishing them. Madison studied the poetry and recommended publishing; however, after starting negotiations with Holt, Mrs. Dewey told Mr. Madison she had decided not to go ahead, on the advice of a family friend, Agnes Meyer.[1] About publication of the poetry, Mrs. Meyer said to Roberta Dewey, "I just have a hunch John wouldn't like it. I think he wrote these poems for his own

---

1. These incidents are related by Charles A. Madison in an oral history interview of 8 November 1967, Special Collections, Morris Library, Southern Illinois University at Carbondale. Agnes Meyer was a journalist, wife of Eugene Meyer, long-time publisher of the *Washington Post,* and mother of the present publisher of the *Post,* Katherine Graham.

private satisfaction and though some of them are very lovely, they are uneven." [2]

From 1957, when Roberta Dewey obtained the poetry, until her death in 1970, she showed the collection to a number of persons who visited her apartment. She had several favorites retyped and mounted, and mended the original manuscripts and typescripts with transparent tape; in addition, she trimmed the margins of many of the sheets of paper and sealed some of them in plastic covers.

By the time the John Dewey Foundation inherited the manuscript collection from the Roberta Dewey Estate in the early 1970s, many students of Dewey's life and writings had heard at least some of the rumors that circulated about the poetry. But facts about the discovery and history of the poetry were nowhere on record. Because more than half the poems were typewritten, with only typewritten or no changes, and because Dewey apparently never acknowledged having written poetry, the Foundation decided to postpone publication of the poems until a thorough study could be made to verify Dewey's authorship and, if possible, to establish when they were composed.

In 1972, the directors of the Foundation undertook first to determine the exact physical history of the poetry. They made inquiries of the surviving Dewey daughters—Jane and Lucy (Mrs. Wolf Brandauer), of Gérard Deledalle, and of Herbert Schneider, Dewey's long-time colleague who moved into Dewey's office when Dewey retired. While that correspondence was in progress, I asked M. Halsey Thomas for all the details he could recall about the background of the poems. The following account summarizes the responses to those various queries. [3]

2. Agnes Meyer to Roberta Dewey, 7 April 1959, John Dewey Papers, Southern Illinois University at Carbondale. Dewey obviously did not intend to publish this poetry. Now, however, some twenty-five years after the death of an important figure like Dewey, it is appropriate that such a significant segment of his writing and life experience should become part of the published record.

3. Letters on which this account is based are: Gérard Deledalle to Sidney Hook, 5 June 1971, 26 January 1973; M. Halsey Thomas to Jo Ann Boydston, 17 January 1973, 11 October 1974; Herbert Schneider to H. S. Thayer, 13 February 1973; Jane Dewey to Sidney Hook, 9 March 1973, all in the private collections of the recipients.

From 1926 to 1928, Thomas was librarian of the Butler Library of Philosophy; access to Dewey's office was through the Library. Thomas wrote me that he was "addicted to Boswellizing," and "usually looked in Dewey's wastebasket at the end of the day, particularly when it was full." He was "rewarded at one time by finding a sheaf of poetry he [Dewey] had written." Thomas wrote in his diary 7 March 1928, "Lately Professor Dewey has been going through some cases of books and papers packed up before he left for China in 1920 or 1921, and I have been gathering up the crumbs, as it were, some things given to me and others saved from his wastebasket.[4] I am probably one of the few—if indeed there are any others—who know that he has actually written poetry, yet I have several things, some in his handwriting, some in his characteristically bad typescript." Thomas added in 1973, "I am sure he did not give me the poetry; that was salvaged from the wastebasket."

In 1939, when Herbert Schneider took possession of Dewey's office, he found a "mess of loose scraps of poetry" in Dewey's roll-top desk. He says he thought the poems quite personal, and, without examining them further, dumped the contents of the drawer in a big wastebasket. When he left the office, he met Thomas in the hall and mentioned throwing away the poetry. Thomas, true Boswellizer, thereupon went to the basket, pulled out the poetry, and preserved it in the Columbiana Collection, where it remained until Mrs. Dewey obtained possession in 1957.

Several years later, Mrs. Dewey also retrieved Deledalle's copies of the poems. Then, following her death in 1970, the poetry—both the originals and Deledalle's copies—went to the John Dewey Foundation.

Thomas's diary entry of 1928 when he first found poetry in Dewey's wastebasket is clear evidence that at least "several things" were written before 1918 when Dewey left New York to go to California and from there to the Orient. Herbert Schneider's 1939 discovery, the drawer "about half full of scraps of poetry," presumably comprised the remaining poems. The accounts of the persons who found the poems,

---

4. Dewey actually left New York earlier, on 25 September 1918, going from California to Japan and on to China in 1919; he returned to New York in October 1921.

Thomas and Schneider, agree, then, that a number of poems—some in Dewey's hand and some in his "characteristically bad typescript"—were in Dewey's desk, that they were preserved by Thomas, that they were all written before 1939, and that several were written before 1918.[5]

Neither of Dewey's surviving daughters was aware of his having written poetry; Jane Dewey suggested that these might be poems her father corrected for any one of a large number of young people he was interested in, but she added that naturally anyone might experiment with writing poetry in the course of a long lifetime.

Curiously, no one asked Dewey himself about the poetry when it was discovered, neither in 1928 nor in 1939. Thomas says that all the materials accumulated in the Columbiana Collection were materials that Dewey "seemed to have no further interest in," and that therefore it "never occurred to us [Thomas and Schneider] to ask for a letter of gift." [6]

A postscript to this account of the discovery and history of the collection of ninety-three typescript and manuscript poems inherited by the John Dewey Foundation from the Roberta Dewey Estate is needed to explain how that collection grew to the total of ninety-eight poems presented in this volume. First, in 1972 when the John Dewey Papers were sorted in the Special Collections of Morris Library at Southern Illinois University at Carbondale, one poem, "Last night I stood upon the hill," was found in the Dewey correspondence and added to the collection. In 1973, Halsey Thomas discovered in his Dewey materials five poems that were not among those the Foundation received from the Roberta Dewey Estate. Those

---

5. Thomas's and Schneider's accounts of the salvaging of the poetry differ in one respect: Thomas says it would have been "too much of a coincidence" for him to have met Schneider in the hall immediately after the poetry had been discarded. He remembers that Schneider put in boxes all the material cleaned out from the desk, material described in Thomas's diary as "all that has survived from his [Dewey's] office." The boxes were stored in the attic of Philosophy Hall and eventually turned over to Columbiana in June 1945 when Schneider expressed concern about the safety of the material. It seems possible that Schneider, being embarrassed by the personal nature of some of the poems, tossed them aside—but in a box rather than a basket. This hypothesis finds some support in Thomas's 1945 diary notation, "Professor Schneider, who turned the material over to us, feels that it should not be made generally available until Mr. Dewey's death."—Thomas to Boydston, 25 February 1976.

6. Thomas to Boydston, 17 January 1973.

five, given by Thomas to the Southern Illinois University Dewey Center and now incorporated into the collection, were among the poems Deledalle saw in 1957; he described them in his handwritten copy, identifying them there, along with one additional manuscript poem, as having been discovered by Thomas in 1928. These are probably the "several things" that Thomas said in his 1928 diary entry were written before Dewey left for the Far East in 1918. Duplicates of three of these five and a variant of one other were in the original Foundation collection; one poem, *In Light,* was not, and it became the second addition to the corpus. Finally, the originals of three poems copied by Deledalle were not in the Foundation collection; these poems appear here as transcribed from Deledalle's copies: a handwritten copy with annotations of one poem, "Athwart the shining gleam," (TMs), and the microfilm of two others—*To a Pedant* (TMs) and "Like formless fog on aimless cruise" (MS).[7]

None of the persons who through the years saw or had possession of the poetry—Schneider, Thomas, Deledalle, Madison, Meyer, Roberta Dewey—doubted that all the poems were composed by John Dewey. Nevertheless, even though the poems were found in Dewey's wastebasket and desk, a collection like this, not published by its author and salvaged years after its composition, must be more than routinely scrutinized for evidences of authorship. That scrutiny follows two general lines: the first is bibliographical, compiling and analyzing information about the physical appearance of the poems and comparing the texts; the second is literary, studying the form and content of the poems and comparing the ideas expressed there with those of Dewey's contemporaneous prose writings. Together these approaches have yielded numerous kinds of evidence that establish beyond reasonable doubt Dewey's authorship of the poems and the approximate dates when they were composed.

Dewey's poems, an important addition to the total body of his work, are presented in clear text; for scholars who want to study changes that Dewey made in his typescripts and manu-

---

7. Because of the large number of untitled poems in the collection that are necessarily referred to by first lines in quotation marks, the convention of putting titles in quotation marks has not been followed here; poem titles appear instead in italics.

scripts, his own alterations and corrections are listed, as are editorial emendations, in the textual apparatus for each poem. The bibliographical evidence is presented in detail in the Textual Apparatus,[8] and briefly summarized here.

Herbert Schneider's description of the physical appearance of the manuscripts and typescripts discovered in Dewey's desk as "a mess of loose scraps of poetry" was accurate: the paper on which the poems appear varies from full-sized sheets to very small torn pieces, with a full range of sizes and shapes between. Of the ninety-eight, only six poems are completely in Dewey's handwriting.[9] Seventy-seven of the remaining ninety-two poems, all typewritten, show indications of composition, alteration, and correction—either at the typewriter or in Dewey's hand, and frequently in both. Most of these changes, additions, and deletions are clear signs of a person at work on his own composition; they consist, as the Apparatus lists of alterations show, of trial lines x'd-out, false starts of both words and lines, post-typing revision in pen and pencil, and variant versions of the same material.

The typewriter faces that appear in the poetry typescripts also appear between 1910 and 1928 throughout Dewey's personally typed letters, notes, and statements, all of which incorporate typewriting peculiarities exactly like those found in the typewritten poetry. Two of these machines were Dewey's own; one, his daughter Evelyn's; two others, used less frequently by Dewey to type material other than poetry, were typewriters that he probably did not own but to which he had regular access. In addition to the identifiable similarities in typewriting between poetry and various kinds of prose, the same patterns of punctuation and spelling characterize both. Even the papers on which most of the poems were typed were also used in typing other materials. Study of the typewriter faces further makes it possible to set limiting dates on the

8. The three chief sources of bibliographical evidence are the John Dewey Papers, the collections of materials at the Center for Dewey Studies, and the large amount of Dewey's personally typed material in the Elsie Ripley Clapp Papers, Southern Illinois University at Carbondale. Elsie Clapp assisted Dewey in several courses he taught at Columbia. During the time she worked with him, Dewey wrote long letters to her, reflecting on and analyzing the course content, primarily in "Psychological Ethics."

9. The three Appendix poems copied by Deledalle are mentioned in distinguishing manuscripts from typescripts; otherwise, they are omitted from tabulations of typewriter faces, papers, and similar matters.

period when the poems were typed, although a number of them may have been composed earlier and retyped; those dates are 1910–18 and 1921–28, with more than three-quarters demonstrably having been typed between 1910 and 1918.

The compilation of the bibliographical evidence just summarized was undertaken to establish Dewey's authorship of the poetry because of the unusual history of the collection and because initially it seemed that Dewey had confided in no one about his extensive experimentation with this mode of expression.[10] Even members of his own family were unaware of his poetic efforts, as comments by his daughters indicate. But several pieces of evidence reveal that Dewey's poetry writing was known to some persons well before Thomas's first find and that Dewey shared poems with at least two of those persons.

A person who saw one of Dewey's poems was his first wife, Alice Chipman Dewey. Corroboration of the handwriting in extensive critical comments on the ribbon copy of *Creation* as Alice Dewey's suggests that they discussed and analyzed this poem,[11] which would be a logical development of their mutual interest in poetry, discovered early in their courtship. The existence of carbon copies of both *Creation* and *A Peripatetic's Prayer* further shows Dewey's intention to share his compositions with another person.

Although he himself never referred anywhere in print or in correspondence to his writing of poetry, Dewey talked about it to Waldo Frank during the time Frank was editor of the short-lived (1916–17) *Seven Arts Magazine*. One of the two articles that Dewey wrote for *Seven Arts*, however, implies that his experiments with poetry were probably then in their peak period, as confirmed by the typewriter evidence. He said there, "Were I a poet, this should be, even at the dangerous risk of com-

10. As noted, Roberta Dewey discussed the poetry with a number of persons after she retrieved it in 1957 from the Columbiana Collection; both M. Halsey Thomas and Herbert Schneider mentioned it also after Dewey's death. The first published reference to these later statements about the poetry seems to be the brief exchange among John Herman Randall, Corliss Lamont, and Herbert Schneider in *Dialogue on John Dewey*, ed. Corliss Lamont (New York: Horizon Press, 1959), p. 49.

11. Jeanne Drew, Drew Consultants, Chicago, Illinois, authenticated the handwriting. In her report to me, she concluded further that comparison of the handwriting on *Creation* with early and late samples of Alice Dewey's handwriting showed that the comments on *Creation* were made at least several years after a sample dated 1906.—Drew to Boydston, 9 April 1975.

parisons invited, an ode. But, alas, the passion as well as the art is lacking." [12] Despite this public disavowal by Dewey of enough poetic passion or poetic art to write an ode—which may actually have been a private joke for Frank—Frank's own writings establish for the record that he knew as early as 1916 about Dewey's poetry. A book of Frank's early *Memoirs,* published only recently, recounts some of his experiences as editor of *Seven Arts.* He writes there: "There was no demarkation between my contacts as an editor and as a man. For instance, I saw John Dewey not only at his office at Columbia University but in his New York apartment and his humble house in Long Island. . . . He confided; yes, he wrote poetry of a sort. Oh, no! it was not to be seen." [13]

Ten years later, writing as "Search-light," Frank figuratively characterized Dewey in his *New Yorker* Profile as a poet—not once, but repeatedly—and mentioned Dewey's poems again:

At heart he is a Christian and a poet: a Christian who will accept no written gospel; a poet who trusts himself to write only on politics and metaphysics. . . . [His disciples] have colored the very action of our world with the thought of this man who wanders through it, lost as a poet, modest as a saint, wistful as an adolescent . . . *His* poems are unpublished; yet his driest work is builded on a mystic faith. . . . If he had revolted deeply from the world, he would have been a lyric poet. . . . If he had been able to find his beauty today in today's world, he would have been a great religious poet. [14]

Frank's reference to *"his* poems" is probably a result of Dewey's earlier confidence rather than of his own direct knowledge of the poems, but awareness of Dewey's poetry may have suggested to him this characterization of Dewey as a poet. [15]

12. John Dewey, "In a Time of National Hesitation," *Seven Arts Magazine* 2 (1917): 3.

13. *Memoirs of Waldo Frank,* ed. Alan Trachtenberg (Boston: University of Massachusetts Press, 1973), p. 89.

14. Frank, "The Man Who Made Us What We Are," *New Yorker* 2 (1926): 15–16.

15. Frank's published references to the Dewey poetry strongly imply that he was not given an opportunity to see any of it; Maxine Greene, now William F. Russell Professor at Teachers College, however, wrote to me that Frank had told her Dewey showed him some of his "excellent and 'very modern' " poems.—Greene to Boydston, 23 April 1975.

Finally, the evidence is incontrovertible that Dewey showed at least two poems to the novelist Anzia Yezierska, a woman with whom he had a romantic relationship during one year, 1917–18. This period will be discussed in some detail later.[16]

From these scattered but solid confirmations that Dewey wrote poetry and that other persons knew about it at the time, it is possible to move to other evidence of his authorship in the content of the poems. Outside the poems that figure in his relationship with Yezierska, only a few biographical references appear. For example, in No. 25, the poet refers to his "loins of fire and head of grey." This "head of grey" expression is like a number of other mentions of the poet's aging that are consonant with the facts of Dewey's life during the "poetry period," concentrated between 1910 and 1918. Similarly linked to Dewey's life during these years are the poetic references to the farm at Huntington, L.I., that the family bought in 1909. These are clearest in *Indian Summer at the Farm*; *In the Country*; "Fair flowers grow in my garden ground"—where he mentions the "grey and ivied wall" that still exists; and in *Two Weeks*, in

16. Lewis S. Feuer was the first person to discover the role and significance of Anzia Yezierska in John Dewey's life. His reference led me to her works that contained the poems providing evidence for his hypothesis that there was an involvement between them. See Feuer, "Dwelling on the Superficial," *New Leader* 57 (1974): 18, where he refers to "the East Side Jewish novelist Anzia Yezierska, with whom Dewey was evidently involved for a time in a romantic relationship" and to the probability that Dewey "eventually wearied of Anzia Yezierska's high-strung temperament."

When I began studying the Dewey poetry for evidences of Dewey's authorship, I was at the same time reading background material for what then seemed completely unrelated research on Dewey's 1918 summer study of the Polish community in Philadelphia. Among the members of Dewey's study group was a Mrs. A. Levitas who served as translator. After J. Christopher Eisele told me that "Mrs. A. Levitas" was the novelist Anzia Yezierska mentioned by Feuer, and that in addition to novels she had written autobiographical material, I began exploring her works for information about her life. In the course of this reading, I discovered in Yezierska's 1932 novel, *All I Could Never Be*, an untitled poem with the first line, "Generations of stifled words reaching out." Two drafts of this poem—typed by Dewey on his own machine and corrected in his hand—are in the Dewey poetry collection. Further reading uncovered a second poem by Dewey in Yezierska's 1950 fictional autobiography, *Red Ribbon on a White Horse*. This poem, the only other one she used in her published writing, is also untitled and opens with the line, "I arise from the long, long night." Starting with these two finds, I was able gradually to unravel the story of the Dewey-Yezierska relationship.

phrases such as "I have a garden of flowers and bees," and, once more, "the wall" that "others built." The most specific and unmistakable biographical reference in any of the poems, however, appears in "To us you came from out of dark," a poem inspired by the successive deaths of the Dewey sons Morris and Gordon. When the Deweys left Ann Arbor, Michigan, they made their first trip to Europe, accompanied by the three young children—Fred, Evelyn, and Morris—before taking up residence at the University of Chicago. In Milan, the youngest child, Morris, died of diphtheria at the age of two and one-half years. Then, when the Deweys' ten-year stay at the University of Chicago ended on a note of disillusionment and frustration, the family made another extended trip to Europe before moving to New York. On this trip, a second son, Gordon, who was then eight years old, contracted typhoid fever and died in September 1904. The Deweys were devastated by these tragedies and Alice never recovered her former vigor. Dewey's poem about the children bears his handwritten date "1905"; in March 1905, he wrote to Alice, "It was just six months ago next Saturday since our light went out." In the poem, also, Gordon, who "came from out of dark / To take the place of him who went—" is "our light," the "brightest of lights that ever shone."

Dewey composed most of these personal and largely private reflections during nine years of the decade 1910–20, the years of his fifties—a difficult enough time for most persons, and one that for Dewey was especially complicated by events related to World War I. Although he hated war, he saw that international approaches to co-operative peaceful action had broken down; his acceptance, first of the nation's military preparedness, and finally of the need for war, alienated some of his most devoted followers. In the name of patriotism, civil rights were frequently infringed throughout the country; his own Columbia University became involved when James McKeen Cattell and Henry W. Dana were fired and Charles Beard resigned in protest.[17] Then, the latter part of this period was

17. For fuller accounts of Dewey's activities during this decade, see Max Eastman, "John Dewey: My Teacher and Friend," *Great Companions* (New York: Farrar, Straus and Cudahy, 1942), pp. 242–98, especially pp. 285–86; and George Dykhuizen, *The Life and Mind of John Dewey* (Carbondale: Southern Illinois University Press, 1973), pp. 153–85.

marked for Dewey by his brief but intense emotional involvement with Anzia Yezierska.

Despite the internal and external stresses of the years between 1910 and 1918, culminating in the frustrations and strains of the Polish study in Philadelphia, this was a most productive time professionally for Dewey. The period opened in 1910 with publication of *How We Think* and moved to the appearance in 1916 of both *Essays in Experimental Logic* and *Democracy and Education,* the work that he said was "for many years that in which my philosophy, such as it is, was most fully expounded." [18] Further, although *Human Nature and Conduct* was not published until 1922, the basic content was organized and delivered in the West Memorial Lectures at Stanford University in 1918. These books are significant landmarks, but the decade also saw voluminous publication of articles on topics ranging from the popular and polemic to the specialized and philosophically technical. Not surprisingly, many of the concerns expressed in these prose works, written during the same period as the poetry, appear as central themes of the poems.

With few exceptions, Dewey's prose writings are restricted to intellectual interests and explorations; critics of his writing style have been legion, and he confessed in 1930 that "thinking and writing have been hard work." But, he explained, "The marks, the stigmata, of the struggle to weld together the characteristics of a formal, theoretic interest and the material of a maturing experience of contacts with realities . . . showed themselves, naturally, in style of writing and manner of presentation." [19] Well before he himself wrote poetry, however, and throughout his life when he wrote about poetry, his prose is imbued with an emotional tone and quality more characteristic of his poetry. [20]

---

18. Dewey, "From Absolutism to Experimentalism," in *Contemporary American Philosophy: Personal Statements,* ed. George P. Adams and Wm. Pepperell Montague (New York: Macmillan Co., 1930), 2:23.

19. Ibid., p. 17.

20. Dewey's earliest discussion of poetry was in "Poetry and Philosophy," *Andover Review* 61 (1891): 105–16, reprinted in *Characters and Events* (New York: Henry Holt and Co., 1929), 1:3–17, with the title, "Matthew Arnold and Robert Browning"; *The Early Works of John Dewey, 1882–1898,* ed. Jo Ann Boydston (Carbondale: Southern Illinois University Press, 1969), 3:110–24.

Considered as a collection, Dewey's poetry is, as Agnes Meyer pointed out, uneven in quality, ranging from random trial lines to polished final versions. This unevenness and the numerous evidences of composition in progress show that many of the poems were not completed.[21] Even though Dewey abandoned a number of poems in the process of composition, a few general observations about the collection are possible. Only nineteen of the ninety-eight poems are completely unrhymed; overall there is a skill in metrics and rhyme beyond what one might expect from an amateur, but also throughout, the emphasis is on content rather than on the formal aspects of poetic composition, clearly more on thought, ideas, and feelings, that is, than on musical appeal. This emphasis on content is particularly apparent in Dewey's tendency to work with stanzas as units of thought, much like verse paragraphs, rather than as strictly formal or musical units.

As it is not possible to determine the chronology of their composition, the ninety-five poems are here arranged, on the basis of content, into four sections, with the three poems no longer in the collection, of which the originals have not been examined, placed in an Appendix. Forty-five poems expressing personal emotion are lyric poems, even though most lack the musical quality usually associated with lyrics. Seventeen

---

See, for example, the following in that article: "The life which the poet presents to us as throbbing, as pregnant, ever new from God, is . . . the genuine revelation of the ordinary day-by-day life of man"—*Early Works* 3:113; "Poetry may deliver truth with a personal and a passionate force which is beyond the reach of theory painting in gray on gray. Indeed, it is the emotional kindling of reality which is the true province of poetry"—*Early Works* 3:112; and, "The great power of poetry to stay and to console . . . is just because of the truth, the rendering of the reality of affairs, which poetry gives us. . . . It is because, amid the conventionalities and make-believes of our ordinary life, poetry flashes home to us some of the gold which is at the very heart and core of our every-day existence, that poetry has its power to sustain us, its sympathy to enhearten us"—*Early Works* 3:122.

21. John Ruskin said, "There are few men, ordinarily educated, who in moments of strong feeling could not strike out a poetical thought, and afterward polish it so as to be presentable"—*Modern Painters*, Vol. III, Pt. IV (New York: John Wiley & Sons, 1878), p. 160n. Dewey was of course more than "ordinarily educated," an experienced writer who wrote, re-wrote, and "polished" material intended for publication; the reader should be reminded, however, that these poems were in fact written primarily for his "personal satisfaction."

poems are nature poems; twenty-eight are philosophical poems and the last five are children's poems.[22] This arrangement is largely an organizational device followed for convenience in editing and discussing the poems. Any such classification is arbitrary to some extent since, apart from the subjectivity of any one reader's judgment in making the clas-

22. The children's poems grouping was made on the basis of style as well as content. These are five poems judged to have been written by Dewey for or about his children, chiefly on the model of Robert Louis Stevenson and Eugene Field.

"John Banding looked and said" is placed among the Children's Poems in part because the simple sing-song ballad form is apparently his only experiment of this kind. As the handwritten compositional changes are clearly in Dewey's hand, it may be hypothesized that he wrote it with or for one of his children, perhaps as a school exercise, or to develop a child's story in verse. The typewriter face is 3, and the typewriting pattern is Dewey's, but in both style and content, "John Banding" is on a considerably more "childish" level than the poems in other groups, as are the remaining four in the Children's Poems.

Like Stevenson in *A Child's Garden of Verses,* Dewey sometimes wrote in the role of a child, when the child was too young or too ill to write for himself. One poem in this group is entitled *This Child's Garden of Verse;* another poem, *A Child's Garden,* in the Lyric Poems, is sophisticated and mature, obviously not a child's poem. But Dewey's use of the title in these two forms argues for close acquaintance with the Stevenson work.

Poems 91 and 95 echo the Stevenson language as well as style: in No. 91, for example, the last two lines, "But father says I only dream / When this all true to me does seem," are on the model of the line in "My Treasures," "For though father denies it, I'm sure it is gold." In No. 95, typed on the same sheet with *This Child's Garden of Verse,* Dewey's image and diction in "Nurse says" are comparable to many in Stevenson; three suffice for illustration: "My bed is like a little boat; / Nurse helps me in when I embark"; "How very big my nurse appeared"; and "Water now is turned to stone / Nurse and I can walk upon." (Robert Louis Stevenson, *A Child's Garden of Verses* [Boston: Herbert B. Turner and Co., 1906], pp. 66, 42, 64, and 65.)

*This Child's Garden of Verse,* although less in the Stevenson mold, is about "Janey," Dewey's youngest daughter, born in 1900. The expression, "Dear sister from my heart," is not taken to indicate that the poem was written by either of Jane's sisters—a possibility strongly denied by Lucy Dewey Brandauer (letter to Jo Ann Boydston, 6 August 1974)—but rather as a typical family appellation used by Dewey. The poem is in typewriter face 1, on Columbia University letterhead paper; it could have been written any time between 1910 and 1918, but the line, "And while she plays and runs so free," implies that the date of composition was early in that period.

Finally, "Next spring earth will be all in green," which is placed in this group, is a different and more polished version of "I should think th'earth would be ashamed." It is included here for easy comparison of the two poems.

sification, many of the poems could be variously categorized in light of varied intents and complex themes.[23]

Broadly viewed, the concerns Dewey expresses in his poetry reflect the "emotions of his heart" or personal responses, and the "moods of his mind" or philosophical interests. The pervasive themes and images of the poems are considered here in those two major groupings. The personal poems, comprising the lyrics and many of the nature poems, are deeply revealing; the philosophical poems, including the remaining nature poems, often treat the same ideas as Dewey's prose, but that similar content, exposed to his poetic imagination, illuminates aspects not only of his thought but quite directly of his emotions as well.

The public image of John Dewey—educational innovator, philosopher, polemicist, political activist—is that of a reserved, serious, unemotional, almost stereotypical New Englander, even though of course it has been widely known that he was a warm family man who gave generously of himself to friends and students. Dewey's poetry taken as a whole neither blurs nor significantly alters this image, but serves rather to expand it with vitally human dimensions. Thoughtful, dignified, and even cool Dewey may have been, but he was also—as we can know him in his poems—loving, sensuous, playful, perceptive, and at times emotionally torn, weary, self-doubting, depressed. His love of nature permeates the poems, almost overshadowing his concern about social interaction and involvement with others, but his understanding of and admiration for his fellow man—his struggles, aspirations, courage—are also dominant themes in the poems.

In the first of the two major groups of poems, the personal ones, the central themes are: love; death; hopes and conflicts; depression and weariness; and the need for rest and peace. Various kinds of love are apparent in the poetry—love of children, of nature, of fellow man, of intelligence, knowledge,

23. Dewey commented on this problem in *Art as Experience* (New York: Minton Balch and Co., 1934), p. 111: "The subject, . . . is outside the poem; the substance is within *it*; rather, *it is* the poem. 'Subject,' however, itself varies over a wide range. It may be hardly more than a label; it may be the occasion that called out the work; or it may be the subject-matter which as raw material entered into the new experience of the artist and found transformation. . . . It is well, then, for the sake of clarity to discriminate not only substance from theme or topic, but both of them from antecedent subject-matter."

truth, and of woman. Only those expressing the love of woman, 1–26, are here called "love poems," inasmuch as the other kinds of love emerge in connection with different central themes.[24] The love poems vary in length from short-line quatrains like *Thoughts* and *When Thou Art Gone,* to the longest poem in the collection, *Two Weeks.* They range widely in mood as well—from the joyous *Thoughts* and the tender *Autumn* to the melancholy *Hope and Memory* and the depressed *The Unending Hours.*

Within this group of poems about a man's love of woman is the special set related to Dewey's involvement with Anzia Yezierska; these poems and Yezierska's semi-factual fiction, written many years later, are the sole surviving records of their relationship. From such records we can only infer specific details of what happened between them; but even though we cannot now reconstruct the complete history of their relationship, Dewey's poems and some of Yezierska's prose—notably two short stories and two novels [25]—enable us to appreciate the emotional depth and intensity of the involvement. This was a significant experience for both of them—and, for her at least, one that she remembered vividly the rest of her life.

Of the thoughts and emotions of Dewey as "man in love," little has been recorded, even in prose, although in the course of his long life, he was more than once a man in love. Characteristically, Dewey never discussed or preserved memorabilia from any relationship he had with a woman. But among the ninety-eight poems he carelessly pushed to the back of a desk drawer and apparently forgot, are several that express the complex responses of a mature John Dewey in love. Now, al-

24. Dewey later explicated his theory about love poetry in *Art as Experience,* pp. 76–77: "If the emotion of love between the sexes had not been celebrated by means of diversion into material emotionally cognate but practically irrelevant to its direct object and end, there is every reason to suppose it would still remain on the animal plane. The impulse arrested in its direct movement toward its physiologically normal end is not, in the case of poetry, arrested in an absolute sense. It is turned into indirect channels where it finds other material than that which is 'naturally' appropriate to it, and as it fuses with this material it takes on new color and has new consequences."

25. "To the Stars," *Century* 102 (May 1921): 65–79 (page references are to the reprint in *Children of Loneliness* [New York: Funk and Wagnalls, 1923], 71–98); "Wild Winter Love," *Century* 113 (February 1927): 485–91; *All I Could Never Be* (New York: Brewer, Warren and Putnam, 1932); and *Red Ribbon on a White Horse* (New York: Charles Scribner's Sons, 1950).

most sixty years later, these poems reveal a deeply moving and hitherto unknown episode in his emotional life that began some months before his fifty-eighth birthday in October 1917 when he met the strikingly handsome thirty-three-year-old writer Anzia Yezierska.[26]

In 1904, Yezierska had received from Teachers College a diploma in domestic science, a field she heartily disliked but one which, because of her limited educational background, was among the few open to her. Having taught domestic science several years, she found herself in 1912 confined at home caring for her infant daughter; she started trying to write then and developed a consuming ambition to become a successful writer. As she became increasingly concerned about broadening her educational background, she constantly sought the acquaintance and assistance of persons who might help her. In 1917, she turned to John Dewey. According to the story she told her daughter many years later, Yezierska knew Dewey by reputation and simply went to his office without an appointment or prior introduction.[27] Her bold venture was a success: she became an auditor in his seminar in social and political philosophy, at a time when non-matriculated persons were not commonly admitted to university classes.[28] During the fall

26. Yezierska's daughter, Louise Levitas Henriksen, spent the summer of 1931 helping her mother prepare for publication the novel *All I Could Never Be*, in which a thinly veiled Dewey-figure appears. Both before and after that summer, Yezierska talked to her from time to time about Dewey. Other members of Yezierska's family whom I interviewed were also aware of her relationship with Dewey. I could not have prepared this account of that relationship without Louise Henriksen's sympathetic assistance; not only has she furnished valuable materials and biographical information, but she has also shared with me her own perceptions of the relationship. One such perception is central: she wrote me in September 1974, "Your study of the poems has, by chance, evoked a fascinating and delicate story about a relationship which illumines facets of Dewey as much as it does my mother."

27. Even though Yezierska told this story late in her life about bracing Dewey in his office, it is supported by her fictional account of many years earlier in which a Yezierska-figure has a similar encounter with the Dewey-figure, "President Irvine," whom she has never met but whose photograph and public demeanor have inspired her.—"To the Stars," *Century* 102 (May 1921): 65–79, reprinted in *Children of Loneliness* (New York: Funk and Wagnalls, 1923), pp. 71–98.

28. Henry Hart, *Dr. Barnes of Merion: A Biography* (New York: Farrar, Straus and Co., 1963), p. 66; William Schack, *Art and Argyrol* (New York: A. S. Barnes and Co., 1960), pp. 102–5.

and spring sessions of 1917–18 when Yezierska attended Dewey's seminar, their romantic relationship developed.

Following the year's seminar, Yezierska and Dewey saw each other infrequently during the summer of 1918 when a group of graduate students [29] conducted under Dewey's leadership a study of conditions in the Polish community of Philadelphia, with Yezierska serving at Dewey's request as translator.[30] Although the $100 monthly stipend was important to her, it was less important than the opportunity to work and associate with Dewey and this group of highly educated persons.

In September of 1918, Dewey left New York for an extended trip to California, Japan, and China, from which he did not return until October of 1921. By the time Dewey took up his post at Columbia again, Yezierska was in Hollywood working on the film production of her first book, *Hungry Hearts*.[31] Thus, Dewey's departure in 1918 effectively ended the period of their closest relationship, but when *Hungry Hearts* was published in 1920, Dewey's name headed the list of distinguished persons to whom Yezierska asked her publisher to send copies.[32]

Yezierska had first sought Dewey out because of his reputation as a man of power and influence, largely unaware that on a personal level she could hardly have chosen better: not only was he intellectually perceptive but he was also a man of com-

29. Dewey listed the participants (all of whom later became recognized figures in American life) and their assignments, as follows: "Brand Blanshard, religious conditions and the activity of the church; Miss Frances Bradshaw, educational conditions, including both public and parochial schools; Mrs. A. Levitas, conditions affecting family life and women; Mr. Irwin Edman began with a study of general intellectual, esthetic and neighborhood activities, but . . . diverted his energies to a study of conditions as affected by international politics. In May, Mr. Barnes asked me to act as adviser and general supervisor of the undertaking."—John Dewey, *Confidential Report on Conditions among the Poles in the United States* (Philadelphia [?]: n.p., 1918), p. 2.

30. Hart, *Dr. Barnes*, pp. 65–67; Schack, *Art and Argyrol*, pp. 102–5; Dewey, *Report on the Poles*, pp. 2–3.

31. *Hungry Hearts* (New York: Houghton Mifflin Co., 1920); *American Film Institute Catalogue of Feature Films 1921–30: Hungry Hearts* F2.2626, Goldwyn Pictures, 26 November 1922.

32. Anzia Yezierska to Mr. Greenslet, 25 October 1920. Houghton Mifflin Publishing Company Records, Houghton Library, Harvard University. The list of names was: "Prof. John Dewey, Young Men's Christian Association, Peking, China; Mr. Henry L. Menken (*sic*), The Smart Set Magazine; Mr. Max Eastman, Masses Magazine; Mr. Louis Untermeyer; Miss Amy Lowell."

passion, a man who by inclination as well as experience, was adept at encouraging and supporting promising persons who needed help.[33] His feeling for Yezierska in time added a special dimension to these qualities, making him warmly sensitive to her particular needs.

By the time Yezierska started to attend Dewey's class, she had already published her first story [34] and was working hard at improving her craft because she felt an intense need to express creatively the experience of her people, the Jewish immigrants in the ghetto. Recognizing that her earlier life in the sweatshops, factories, and tenements had provided her with rich material for stories "unutterable by me and mine," and recognizing at the same time that she lacked confidence, Dewey wrote for her a poem expressing reassurance and warm support, as well as wistful recognition of the several kinds of distance that separated them:

> Generations of stifled worlds reaching out
> Through you,
> Aching for utt'rance, dying on lips
> That have died of hunger,
> Hunger not to have, but to be.
>
> Generations as yet unuttered, dumb, smothered,
> Inchoate, unutterable by me and mine,
> In you I see them coming to be,
> Luminous, slow revolving, ordered in rhythm.
> You shall not utter them; you shall be them,
> And from out thy pain
> A great song shall fill the world.
>
> And I from afar shall see,
> As one watching sees the star
> Rise in the waiting heavens,
> And from the distance my hand shall clasp yours,

33. As Sidney Hook has said, "Dewey encouraged and over-encouraged many who showed a glint of promise. Whatever the quality of their work, they achieved more because of his apparent faith in them. . . . There was a simplicity and trustfulness about him, almost a calculated naïveté in his relations with people whose ulterior motives were rather transparent. It was as if he were aware of the many ways a person could deceive or disappoint him and yet made that person feel he had perfect confidence in him. He bet on people and was rarely let down."—"Some Memories of John Dewey," *Commentary* 14 (1952): 247.

34. "The Free Vacation House," *Forum* 54 (December 1915): 706–14.

> And an old world be content to go,
> Beholding the horizons
> Tremulous with the generations
> Of the dawn.[35]

Dewey's empathy with Yezierska's desire for expression and with her difficulties—"thy pain"—shows clearly here, but so too does a poignant restraint, reflected in his expressions, "I from afar shall see," and "from the distance my hand shall clasp yours."

Of Dewey's poems for Yezierska, it is certain only that she saw "Generations" and one other because these are the two she used in her published work; the second is "I wake from the long, long night." There, Dewey is in turn asking understanding and support, with overtones suggesting a love that is not to be fulfilled. This poem explicitly recognizes the contrasts between them, especially the contrast between her freedom and the more established, duty-bound, routinized pattern of his own life; he says he keeps his eyes earthward, "lest the beauties / Of a life not yet trammeled distract / My ordered paces from the path / . . . and the wrath / Of stern-eyed freedom break the chains / Which keep me from the wilderness of tears." He accepts his responsibilities, even though the "silken web" of duties that binds him sometimes leaves him feeling cut off from real emotion—"joyless, griefless":

> I wake from the long, long night
> Of thoughtless dreams, fancies
> Nor pleased nor vexed. And despite
> The sleep of untroubled trances
> Joyless, griefless, begins the round
> Of day's unillumined duties,
> A silken web in which I'm bound.

In another poem, *The Round of Passion*, which is a sort of extended Lucretian metaphor of a love relationship, he sounds the same note of melancholy at the end, "All as before. / The weary way is trod." Precisely because Dewey's own life was

---

35. The originals of many poems printed here without indentions have an irregularly slanting indention with no discernible pattern, probably because Dewey seldom set margin stops on his typewriters. The first line in both Dewey's drafts of "Generations" uses "worlds"; Yezierska's published versions use "words."

based on "ordered paces," and because he was unwilling to "break the chains" that bound him, he resisted yielding to his feelings for Yezierska. In his poem *Two Weeks,* he exclaims, "Renounce, renounce; / The horizon is too far to reach. / All things must be given up. / Driest the lips, when most full the cup."

Judging as we now must from photographs and the accounts of those who knew her, Yezierska was vibrant and vital, excitable and exciting.[36] She was an attractive woman, with a vivid personality that intensified the effects of her arresting looks—abundant red hair, velvet white skin, and large blue-green eyes. Even as he acknowledged the difficulties created by his emotions toward her, Dewey saw Yezierska in his poem "There stirred within me" as a symbol of "the ghosts of many a love." In the voices of those earlier loves, he describes her:

> For all we might have been
> Eternally is she:
> The surprise of the flushed welcome of the day
> After th'encompassing mystery of night,
> The tender twilight creeping to the sky's last ray,
> The certain faith the new born day doth plight
> To each unsullied hour that eager comes to be,
> The greatness of whatever's unpossest and free
> Like the glory of the unbought comradeship of earth and sea.

At first, the old loves say, "You shall not let our sister in / To stifle in this sepulcher / Where from dumb death we now murmur." They swear this

> By the sweetness of every chance caress,
> By the words of love we swore,
> By the quick magic of each vagrant tress,
> And every sigh that from sealèd lips did pour,
> By every intercepted glance
> That spoke the untold tale,
> By every touch of hands that did enhance
> Desire till distance lost its stern avail,
> By the drops of blood that trait'rous started

36. The "excitable and exciting" characterization is Louise Henriksen's, in a letter of 4 March 1975. Her fuller description of her mother's personality in that letter is: "She was a dazzling, stunning volcano of a person who made an overwhelming impression on some people. . . . She was romantic, impatient, childlike, excitable and exciting."

> In warm wonder whene'er we met,
> By every ling'ring kiss with which we parted,
> By every sacred tear that wet
> Th'innocence of our unopened scroll of love,
> By every laughing joy that illumined
> With the glow of all the stars above
> That scroll when its pages opened.

But at the close of the poem, the old, unrealized loves recognize and tenderly declare that "In her we yet shall live, / To her our unlived lives we give." [37]

Although this poem, and *Two Weeks*—the longest and most intensely personal in the whole collection—were inspired by Yezierska, she may never have seen them. That they were among the others in the collection may mean that he simply never sent or gave them to her. It is also possible, however, that they were there because she returned them to him; she says fictionally that she returned all the letters the Dewey-figure sent her. The slight differences between her version of "Generations" and Dewey's drafts suggest that she may have seen a third recopied version of that poem.

Dewey's recognition of the temporary and peripheral nature of any involvement he might have with Yezierska is clearly reflected in his lines in *Two Weeks*: "What I am to any one is but a loan / From those who made, and own," those with whom he has "loved, and fought." Even among the intimate glimpses in the poetry of his deepening feeling for her, notes of caution and control also emerge, reflecting his realistic assessment of himself and his situation. Yezierska must at some point, however obliquely, have questioned whether he was overly concerned about protecting his safe life, symbolized by honors, or possessions. *Two Weeks* opens with his response:

> Riches, possessions hold me? Nay,
> Not rightly have you guessed
> The things that block the way,

37. Unlike *Two Weeks*, which has numerous internal references to identify Yezierska, "There stirred within me" could have been written to any woman Dewey loved. The physical evidence that Yezierska inspired it, however, is compelling: it is in the same typeface, 4, as "Generations" and "I wake"; those two poems, *Two Weeks*, and "There stirred within me" are all on Efficiency Bond paper—four of only sixteen in the entire collection on that particular paper.

Nor into what ties I've slowly grown
By which I am possest.
For I do not own.

Who makes, has. Such the old old law.
Owned then am I by what I felt and saw
But most by them with whom I've loved, and fought,
Till within me has been wrought
My power to reach, to see and understand.
Such is the tie, such the iron band.

His feeling for her, then, caused him to cast his family and other obligations in the role of an "iron band." But his recognition of both their situations further included his awareness of the contrast in ages: he was approaching sixty and she was still in her early thirties. He alluded to this awareness in several poems; in *Two Weeks,* he explains the import of the age disparity:

Then there's that matter of youth and age.
Youth's felicitous, undaunted rage
For living against long years age has spent
In bare existence, till there remains
But stored up memories in detachment
From the things that might have been, and stains
Of things that should not have been and are—
The choked up fountain and th'uneffacèd scar.

Then too there is the long drawn experience
Of age. You say you have lived longer and most.
Truly, if you measure by what is deep and tense—
The only scale of quick youth. But if by the host
And unnumbered diversity by which age counts
Rather than passions few and deep, then not so.

He could, however, be light-hearted about such an important consideration, as in *Time Laid Low,* where he quixotically suggests that love can overcome even this obstacle:

Time with his old flail
  Beat me full sore;
Till: Hold, I cried,
  I'll stand no more.

Then heard I a wail
  And looking spied

> How love's little bow
> Had laid time low.

In *The Round of Passion,* a more serious allusion to his years, it is not "love's little bow" that conquers age, but the fire of passion:

> Through slow dull years
> The sun did turn to wood
> Barren and cold.
> Till in sudden instant
> The mystery of sun
> (Lurked hidden in the wood)
> Returned to pristine fire.
> Consumed in flame
> The old was young.

Despite caution and control, despite realistic objectivity about the obstacles to any deeper involvement between them, Dewey reveals in *Two Weeks* that his emotions have led him to question even the authenticity of his own responses: are they "mimic passions" or are they "authentic heaven and hell"?

> Damn fiction, damn romance.
> Since I have read, I shall never know
> Whether in an ancient mirror I see prance
> Before me mimic passions in a row,
> Or if they are authentic heaven and hell.
> Moreover no one can ever tell.

So it is that in spite of the "iron band" of the long-standing relationships that hold him, he acknowledges his complete absorption in thoughts of her:

> Yet would I have you know
> How utterly my thoughts go
> With you to and fro
> In a ceaseless quest,
> Half annoy
> And all a blessed joy.

He thinks about Yezierska writing alone in her room, and about the pleasantly disturbing effects of her unpredictability:

> Does she now think or write or rest?
> What happens at this minute—it's just eight—
> Has she written or shall I wait

In sweet trouble of expectancy
For some fresh wonder yet to be? [38]
Whate'er, howe'er you move or rest
I see your body's breathing
The curving of your breast
And hear the warm thoughts seething.

Her living conditions in the tenement [39] and her struggles to rise above them cause Dewey to say, "I watch the lovely eyes that visions hold / Even in the tortured tangles of the tenement / Of a life that's free and bold."

In her writings, Yezierska frequently uses the expression "cold in the heart, clear in the head," to characterize puritan Anglo-Saxons.[40] She probably teasingly told Dewey she found him so, since in *Two Weeks* he gently rejects the label in his line, "So at least she said," while the warmth and *tendresse* of the poem itself effectively belie her charge. He remembers holding her hand, and dreams that she is near:

While I am within this wonder
I am overcome as by thunder
Of my blood that surges
From my cold heart to my clear head—
So at least she said—
Till my body sinks and merges
In communion with the wine and bread.

---

38. Dewey probably used in conversation an expression similar to the "fresh wonder" of his poem: in *All I Could Never Be,* Yezierska has the philosopher Henry Scott say to the Polish translator Fanya Ivanowna, "You make life full of daily wonder" (p. 65).

39. Even though Yezierska did not live in the tenements after she first moved out as a young woman, she continued to identify herself with the life there both in "fact" and in fiction.

"I left my home and went to live [at 21] in a tenement room for which I paid seven dollars a month."—"My Ambitions at 21 and What Became of Them," *American Hebrew* 25 (August 1922): 342, 358.

"How far away was that dark hole in the tenements whence I came."—"A Hungry Heart and $10,000," *Literary Digest* 87 (1925): 46. See also *Hungry Hearts,* p. 226; *Children of Loneliness,* pp. 76–77; *Bread Givers* (New York: Doubleday Page and Co., 1925), p. 158.

40. Among Yezierska's many uses of this contrast to describe "Anglo-Saxons," five occur in *Salome of the Tenements* (New York: Boni and Liveright, 1923), pp. 110, 112, 143, 148, 212; one in *Red Ribbon on a White Horse,* p. 123; and in *All I Could Never Be,* it appears as "Americans with their cold hearts and clear heads" (p. 37).

As in his disclaimer, "Were I a poet," so, too, in *Two Weeks,* he says to Yezierska, "I told you my diet should be prose," and, "These words of mine make no poesy." But he goes on to explain to her his reasons for making the poetic attempt:

> I told you my diet should be prose.
> I did not know there would always float
> Before my sight the waving lily and the beckoning rose,
> Or that even on the city's hard paved streets
> My thoughts should ever shape themselves into a boat
> To bear you on every wind that blows
> The hopes and fears that measure out the beats
> Of the blood that pulses from my heart.
>
> Perhaps this mixture is the better art.
> You said my logic you could never grasp,
> While my poetic words—thus you blessed them—
> Would fall like manna on a hung'ring soul.

About "these words" of his that "make no poesy," Dewey tells her,

> They rasp,
> Like the harsh divisions of my mind. But invest them
> With your own beauty and their final goal
> Shall be more than prose. The mixture uncouth
> Shall then speak to you the very truth
> Of me, the broken parts of an ineffectual whole.

However fleeting or short-lived may have been the emotion that inspired this gloomy introspection, its impact on Dewey was surely considerable. But whatever self-doubt or questioning may have led him to say that "the very truth" of his being is "the broken parts of an ineffectual whole," was soon countered, and he concludes the poem with a more balanced and revealing look at himself:

> Then take me as I am,
> Partly true and partly sham
> Not from wilful choice
> But by too ready acceptance
> Of the constraining work of chance,
> Here a blow to shape, there a luring voice
> To call. If I have not wholly stood
> Neither have I wholly bent.
> Just th'usual mixed up mess of bad and good
> I bring to you as it was sent.

Two of the remaining poems that seem likely to have stemmed from Dewey's feeling for Yezierska—*Autumn* and *Natural Magic*—illustrate especially well his use of nature images, not only in the love poetry but also in poems expressing the full range of his thought and emotions.[41] As if writing about his own poetry, Dewey later described in *Art as Experience* how poets use nature images to show love: "Consult the poets, and we find that love finds its expression in rushing torrents, still pools, in the suspense that awaits a storm, a bird poised in flight, a remote star or the fickle moon. . . . Verbal expression may take the form of metaphor, but behind the words lies an act of emotional identification, not an intellectual comparison" (p. 76).

*Autumn,* one of the most polished of the poems, with metric and stanzaic patterns more strictly imposed, can be assumed to be about Yezierska, who is the "child of fall." Since Yezierska never knew her exact birth date, throughout her life she celebrated the anniversary, by her own decision, in October.[42] The "white" images invoked in this poem are particularly appropriate for her, as a number of persons who knew her remember vividly the impact of her exceptionally creamy white skin. In *Autumn,*

> fair and white in soul is she
> Like the white wonder that lights up space
> When sudden blooms th'apple tree
> That yields itself acquist.

Other metaphors that Dewey attributes to "the poets" in their expressions of love appear in another expression of his own love, *Natural Magic,* where the beloved—probably Yezierska again—is depicted as

> wed
> By nature's mystic marriage pledge

---

41. In his earliest published statement on poetry, Dewey said, "Man need not simply look to nature for encouragement in bearing the burden of the world, for strength to be like her, self-poised, self-dependent. Man may rejoice in her every pulse of life, having the conviction that in her life he, too, lives; knowing that her every event furthers some deed of his, knowing that her beauty is the response to some aspiration of his."—"Poetry and Philosophy," *Early Works* 3:121.

42. In her records at Teachers College, she listed her birth date as 19 October 1883.

> To changing seasons; scents of soil;
> Luminous mists by the dim edge
> Of earth's horizon; to the coil
> Of unsubstantial clouds brightened
> By intangible lights of crescent moons.

The typewriter faces in several other love poems appear in non-poetry materials during the time Dewey knew Yezierska; these poems might, on that evidence alone, have been inspired by her.[43] In these, too, nature images predominate. Dewey's "still pool" illustration in *Art as Experience* appears in *Thy Mind* as "A pool of clear waters thy mind, / Sunlit, unrippled by any wind." His "bird poised in flight," is in *Thoughts,*

> Glad at birth, nestled on earth
> Silk'n doves of joy—
> Hover'd on high, to thee they fly
> Dear Love's decoy.

The "remote star" is a clear feature of *In Light,* as "Heaven's one star / Beloved afar." His "rushing torrents" are "Flowing from some snow capped mountain peak," to feed the depths of "thy mind." And in the delicately wrought *Song,* nature images are used to show "How joy may spring from former quarrel," when

> To blandness melts the chillèd sky;
> In brightness buds the ash grey laurel.

Unlike Dewey's responses to his relationship with Yezierska, which are recorded in the poems quoted here and all written within a one-year period, Yezierska's writings about him and about her feeling for him are extensive and dispersed

43. Several poems that might, by reason of content, seem also to have been inspired by Anzia Yezierska must be excluded because the two typefaces that appear in them were no longer in use when he met her in 1917; they are: *Hope and Memory,* "Is this the end?", *My Body and My Soul, One Night, Ties,* and *The Unending Hours.* Similarly, love poems in which no references identify Yezierska, but which, because the typewriter faces were in use during the time he knew her, might have been written for her are: *In Light, Song, Swinburnian, Thoughts, Thy Mind, Time Laid Low, Two Joys,* and the recopied version of *When Thou Art Gone,* entitled *Absence.* One manuscript poem may have been to her—"Empty as high heaven's heartless shell"; two other typewritten poems, if interpreted as extended metaphors of a love relationship, might also be linked to Dewey's experience with Yezierska: *The Round of Passion* and *Romance.*

in material published during a period of thirty-two years. To complete the account of their involvement, it is necessary to digress briefly from the discussion of Dewey's poetic themes and images to examine her depictions of Dewey and of their relationship in those writings.

When Dewey left New York in 1918, Yezierska enrolled in an extension course on writing at Columbia University. "The Miracle," [44] her first story published after the course was finished, marks the beginning of her use of the Dewey *persona* and life in her writings—a practice she followed throughout her work, gradually adding and embroidering details about him, about herself, and about their relationship. [45]

Most of her writings are to some extent autobiographical, and all her fiction has connections in fact; conversely, contemporary published accounts of events in her life—based on interviews with her—are dubiously factual: she fictionalized her own biography, at different times altering dates and especially the account of her age. The numerous inconsistencies in newspaper stories, reviews, and articles about her attest to her imaginative reconstructions. [46]

Yezierska referred often to the urgency of her desire to

44. "The Miracle," *Metropolitan* 50 (1919): 29–30, 66–68.

45. Early depictions of "Dewey" traits appear in "The Miracle"; "Hunger," *Harper's* 140 (1920): 604–11; "Wings," *McCalls* 57 (1920): 46–47, 50–51.

46. For example, she said to W. Adolphe Roberts, as to other interviewers, "Sonya Levien of the *Metropolitan Magazine* was the first editor to accept a manuscript from me." (Interview with Roberts, "My Ambitions," p. 342.) Her first story, "The Free Vacation House," was, as mentioned, published four years earlier than the *Metropolitan* story. Cf. *Twentieth Century Authors,* ed. Stanley J. Kunitz and Howard Haycraft (New York: H. W. Wilson, 1942), p. 1563, "She began to write short stories of Ghetto life in 1918."

Yezierska had married Arnold Levitas in 1911; her daughter, Louise, was born in 1912. *Twentieth Century Authors,* however, says in 1942, "Miss Yezierska—she is unmarried—," p. 1563.

The matter of age was the most flexible. *Twentieth Century Authors* lists her birth date as 1885 and says the family immigrated to New York in 1901. But in 1901 Yezierska was in her second year at Teachers College; in her Teachers College records, she listed her birth date as 19 October 1883. Further, compare those dates with Edythe H. Browne's statement in her interview with Yezierska (*Bookman* 58 [1923]: 270), "She emigrated from Poland to America when she was nine years old." See the discussion of her various "ages" in the text. Even the members of her family were not sure how old she was, and the *New York Times* obituary (23 November 1970) reported that she was "about ninety."

write, and described the rebuffs she encountered because of her difficulties with the English language. In "To the Stars," she (as Sophie Sapinsky) is told by a college dean, " 'My dear child,'—Dean Lawrence tried to be kind,—'the magazine world is overcrowded with native-born writers who do not earn their salt. What chance is there for you, with your immigrant English?' " (p. 71). She then turns to the head of the English department, telling him, "For me, it's a case of life or death. I got to be a writer." He will not accede to her request to take "every course in English and literature from the beginning to the end," because, he says, "in order to be eligible for our regular college courses, you would have to spend two or three years in preparation" (pp. 72–73).

As she leaves his office, however, she encounters the president of the college, a character based on Dewey. "For one swift instant Sophie looked into kindly eyes. 'Could he understand? Should I cry out to him to help me?' " (p. 73). But she is afraid to talk to him. Instead, she goes back to her lonely rented room, where "every nerve within her cried aloud with the gnawing ache of her unlived life."

"Must I always remain buried alive in the black prison of my dumbness? Can't I never learn to give out what's in me?" Centuries of suppression, generations of illiterates clamored in her: "Show them what's in you! If you can't write it in college English, write it in 'immigrant English!' "

The catalog had fallen open at the photograph of the president. There looked up at her the one kind face in the heartless college world. The president's eyes gazed once more steadily into hers (pp. 74–75). . . . The calm faith of the eyes leveled steadily at her seemed to rebuke her despair. The sure faith of that lofty face lifted her out of herself. . . . The understanding eyes seemed to pour vision into her soul (p. 79).

In response to his "calm faith," she seizes the vision and begins to write. "Her power seemed to come from some vast, fathomless source. The starved passions of all the starved ages poured through her in rhythmic torrent of words—words that flashed and leaped with the resistless fire of youth burning through generations of suppression" (p. 84).

As Yezierska says in her fiction, Dewey was in fact able to inspire self-confidence in her; his sympathy and support were key factors in that inspiration. Like another Dewey-based character in "Wild Winter Love," "he was a man of brains who understood the warm, rich muddle of her experience" (p. 490). Comparison of the Yezierska passages quoted above with Dewey's paean of faith and encouragement, the poem "Generations," can serve to illustrate the frequently remarkable reflections of his poetry in her prose.

Yezierska offered to Houghton Mifflin in 1920 a poem she said "would go well with the suggested volume of short stories entitled Hunger." The poem was undoubtedly "Generations." But she had second thoughts about the propriety of her offer and some two weeks later she wrote again, saying, "Please return the poem I gave you with the mss. I must first get Prof. Dewey's permission to use it in any way." [47] Twelve years later, she published "Generations" in her novel *All I Could Never Be*, along with her version of how he came to write the poem. There is no record that she sought or obtained Dewey's permission to use the poem there, but of course she was fully aware that he would not claim authorship. Part of this novel is a fictionalized account of the 1918 Polish study; long before the group leaves for Philadelphia, Fanya Ivanowna, translator for the research team, is attracted to Henry Scott, the philosopher who is to be in charge of the work:

. . . she had thought of so much she wanted to write to him, but in her room, when she put pencil to paper, she could only wrest out of herself one line—a line without beginning and without end.

"Generations of stifled words—reaching out to you—aching for utterance—dying on my lips unuttered—"
. . . . . . . . . . . . . . . . . . . . . . . . . . . . . . . . . . . . . . . . . . . . . . . . . . . . . . . . .
When the letter was pushed under her door, . . . she tore it open hastily. There was a poem inside . . . a poem based on the rhythm and phrasing of the line she had written.

"Generations of stifled words, reaching out *through you*
  Aching for utterance, dying on lips
That have died of hunger,
  Hunger not to have, but to be" (pp. 41–43).

The rest of the poem appears at that point in the novel and is repeated—except for the last stanza—as Fanya remembers it later in life (p. 214).

47. Yezierska to Greenslet, 3 April 1920 and 20 April 1920. Houghton Mifflin Records, Harvard University.

In all Yezierska's stories, the Dewey-like characters provide strong support and understanding to the Anzia-like characters. In "Wild Winter Love," the ghetto novelist Ruth Raefsky says to a friend about an older man, a lawyer whom she loves: "My writing is but a rushing fountain of song to him. I pour myself out at his feet, in poems of my people, their hopes, their dreams. He listens to me with the wonder of a child listening to adventure. It's all so fresh and new to him, my world, that it becomes fresh and new to me" (p. 490). In "To the Stars," Sophie says to President Irvine: "The turning-point in my life is to know I got a friend. I owe it to the world to do something, to be something, after this miracle of your kindness" (p. 95). Years later, in *Red Ribbon on a White Horse,* the writer-heroine thinks about John Morrow, and remembers that "He saw my people in me, struggling for a voice" (p. 30).

Dewey's recognition of Yezierska's talent, his confidence in her abilities, and his continuing support helped her gain handsome rewards, but, ironically, not until he was in the Orient, half a world away: in 1920, her story "The Fat of the Land" [48] was selected as the "best of the best" short stories of 1919 for O'Brien's *Best Short Stories of 1919.* [49] Screen rights to *Hungry Hearts,* the collection of her stories that she published in 1920, brought her $10,000 and the work became a movie in 1922.

Yezierska, like Dewey, was very much aware of the discrepancy in age between them and even exaggerated it in both her fullest accounts of their relationship, where she shows Henry Scott and John Morrow as sixtyish, Fanya Ivanowna and herself as twenty-three. Her 1950 work, *Red Ribbon on a White Horse,* openly autobiographical and written in the first person, [50] is a revealing example of her usual conflation of fact and fiction. Many well-known figures such as Elinor Glyn, Sam Goldwyn, Rupert Hughes, Richard Wright, and Will Rogers appear in this book under their own names; only "John Morrow," the lawyer with whom Yezierska has a romance is, as

48. "The Fat of the Land," *Century* 98 (August 1919): 466–79; reprinted in *Hungry Hearts,* pp. 178–223.

49. O'Brien, Edward J., ed., *Best Short Stories of 1919* (Boston: Small, Maynard and Co., 1920).

50. W. H. Auden in his "Introduction" refers to the book as "autobiography," and it was so advertised by the publisher.

Dewey said of himself in *Two Weeks,* "partly true and partly sham." In this work there is an incident—perhaps a fiction within a fiction—exemplifying how and why she frequently seemed to be shifting facts about her age: the chief of publicity for Goldwyn Studios asks Yezierska how old she is. She replies that she does not know. When the inquiry is repeated, she cries out in embarrassment,

"I don't know my age. My mother had too many children, too many worries for bread, to keep track of when we were born."
He looked me over appraisingly. "I'd say you were about thirty-five."
"I'll say I am about thirty," I said (p. 80).

Yezierska's fictional exaggeration of the difference in age between herself and Dewey offers, however, a key to her image of him; though the difference was at least twenty-five years, the disparity was even greater for her in the sense that he was her father, her Pygmalion, her god.[51] The matter of age difference is ever-present in the four Yezierska works detailing her relationship with Dewey and is discussed by both male and female characters. In "To the Stars," Sophie Sapinsky goes to the apartment of President Irvine to thank him for his support and encouragement. As they sit talking about writing and about education, he tells her "his dream of democracy in education, of the plans under way for the founding of the new school." He says in part:

Teachers, above all others, have occasion to be distressed when the earlier idealism of welcome to the oppressed is treated as a weak sentimentalism; when sympathy for the unfortunate and those who have not had a fair chance is regarded as a weak indulgence fatal to efficiency. The new school must aim to make up to the disinherited masses by conscious instruction, by the development of personal power for the loss of external opportunities consequent upon the passing of our pioneer days.

President Irvine's "dream and plan" sound Deweyan, and indeed they should: the passage is a long verbatim quotation without acknowledgment from John Dewey's 1916 address to

51. This insight was also expressed by Louise Henriksen in her letter of 9 July 1975 to me.

the National Education Association.[52] But, the fictional President Irvine adds, in an oblique reference to his age: "I shall never see the America which is to be. . . . It will not come in my day. But I have seen its soul like a free wild bird, beating its wings not against bars but against the skies that the light might come through and reveal the earth to be" (*Children of Loneliness*, p. 97). In another story treating the age disparity, Ruth Raefsky, a neighbor of the narrator in "Wild Winter Love," becomes a famous Jewish ghetto novelist, "the New Voice of the East Side." She suffers a period of depression, but when the narrator sees her next, she is radiant. Her friend asks in astonishment, "You—at forty-seven, in love?" She replies, "Yes. And with a man even older than I. What does youth know about love?" (p. 489). The Dewey character, Henry Scott, tells Fanya Ivanowna, "It is you who suffer, while happiness comes to me. You who are young and powerful, alive for the world, and should have the world alive in you. While in my twilight, a beautiful garden with the brightness and perfume distilled from all the ages, is suddenly opened to me" (*All I Could Never Be*, p. 58).

In Dewey's poem "I wake from the long, long night," he had referred to the "stern-eyed freedom" that might

> turn me loose to suffer in the lanes
> Of thorn trees unpossessed as yet by man,
> From which no harvest shall I reap
> Save stabs and flames of pain, and wan
> Exhaustions among th'unshepherded sheep
> Of thoughts which travel th'untracked wild
> Of untamed desire.

Years later, when Yezierska wrote *All I Could Never Be*, she remembered the striking "unshepherded sheep" metaphor and used it in her prose as "unshepherded sheep of thought lost in trackless wilds of untamed desire" (p. 108). Then, after eighteen more years had passed, she incorporated into *Red Ribbon* her version of Dewey's poem, which she says John Morrow sent her while on a business trip to Chicago. In both *Red Ribbon* and *All I Could Never Be*, Yezierska wrote that the Dewey-figure made this business trip to Chicago fairly early

52. "Nationalizing Education," *Journal of the National Education Association* 1 (1916): 187.

in their relationship (*All I Could Never Be*, p. 57; *Red Ribbon on a White Horse*, p. 111). The evidence shows that Dewey, in fact, made trips to Chicago both in December 1917 and in January 1918. Yezierska's rendition of Dewey's poem is unrhymed, more concentrated and less conventional than his original:

> I arise from a long, long night of thoughtless
>     dreams
> Joyless, griefless begins the web of unillumined
>     duties
> A silken web in which I'm bound.
>     Earthward my eyes,
> Lest your spirit keep me from the pact with my
>     possessions
> And lure me to your wilderness of tears,
> Where no harvest shall I reap, save stabs and
>     flames of pain
> And wan exhaustion, among the unshepherded
>     sheep of thought
> Who travel through trackless wilds of untamed
>     desire. (*Red Ribbon on a White Horse*, pp. 111–12.)

Yezierska's feelings for John Dewey—or at least for her own complex image of him—suffuse her writings. She says in *Red Ribbon*, "If I had never met him I would have dreamed him into being" (p. 113), and in some respects, she did "dream him into being." She acknowledges in *All I Could Never Be* that "her swift imagination went on creating him in the image of her own desire" (p. 31). Even though "she looked at him in blind hero-worship" (*All I Could Never Be*, p. 34), however, her image was not of a one-dimensional flawless being. She often depicts a Dewey-figure as the Anglo-Saxon or Gentile struggling to overcome the Puritanism that made him "cold in the heart, clear in the head," and she has one of the Polish study group ask, "I wonder what the old man is like personally?" " 'No one knows him personally,' put in Miss Foster. 'He's as dry and dull and bloodless as he is at his seminars' " (*All I Could Never Be*, p. 84). But throughout this scene, in which all the group members gossip about "the old man," Fanya listens to their malicious comments with contempt: none of them knows him as she does; she has found ardor and tenderness beneath the typically restrained exterior.

In Yezierska's characterization, Dewey is the intellectual New Englander; she is the exotic Oriental. The attraction of opposites—Anglo-Saxon and Slav, Gentile and Jew—is an important aspect of her treatment of her relationship with Dewey.

Now and then threads of gold have spun through the darkness—links of understanding woven by fearless souls—Gentiles and Jews—men and women who were not afraid to trust their love.

It's because he and I are of a different race [53] that we can understand one another so profoundly, touch the innermost reaches of the soul, beyond the reach of those who think they know us.

Outwardly my lover is one of those cold reasonable Anglo-Saxons. . . . A respectable citizen. Devoted to his wife. Adores his children. We're drawn to each other by something even more compelling than the love of man for woman, and woman for man. It's that irresistible force as terrible as birth and death that sometimes flares up between Jew and Gentile ("Wild Winter Love," pp. 489–90).

A feature of Yezierska's presentation of Dewey as "outwardly cold and reasonable" is her criticism of his writing style, criticism she uses to sharpen the contrast between her earthiness and his intellectuality. In her 1921 review of *Democracy and Education* in *Bookman,* an article that marks the only time Yezierska referred to Dewey by name in print, she says, "Unfortunately, Professor Dewey's style lacks flesh and blood. It lacks that warm personal touch that would enable his readers to get close to him. He thinks so high up in the head that only the intellectual few can follow the spiraling point of his vision." [54] Later, the same comment—about the same book—is put in the mouth of Fanya Ivanowna in *All I Could Never Be*: Fanya tells Henry Scott, "Your book on 'The Meaning of Democracy' belies the title. It's written in such abstract, undemocratic language nobody but a handful of college people can make head or tail out of it" (p. 70). She has Sophie Sapinsky tell President Irvine, "Your language is a little too high over my head for me to understand what you're talking about"

53. Yezierska often characterizes Jews and Gentiles (or Anglo-Saxons) as of "different races," a somewhat more jarring note today than in her own lifetime.
54. "Prophets of Democracy," *Bookman* 52 (1921): 497.

(p. 96). Her fictional and non-fictional references to the abstractness of his thought echo Dewey's statement in *Two Weeks*, "You said my logic you could never grasp."

Still another dimension of Yezierska's image of Dewey is apparent in the way she interprets his perception of her. One of the Polish study group complains to Henry Scott that Fanya Ivanowna "has no sense of proportion—no shading—no discrimination. . . . She's just one red, hot fire of emotion." " 'Yes,' Henry admitted. 'She is one red, hot fire. And where would we be without fire? What do sensible people do with fire? They don't turn their backs on it and go away. They try to get some of its vital heat and yet not get burned up by it' " (*All I Could Never Be*, pp. 96–97).

In this Henry Scott depiction Yezierska conveys the rumors persisting into our own time that not only was Dewey the cool, grey, dignified figure of his public image but that he was also, even in later years, extremely attractive to women of all ages. He was a man of presence, powerful intellect, human sympathy, instant international recognition; each of these qualities alone would suffice to attract many women, and the combination seems to have been irresistible to some. Yezierska has one of the Polish study workers report, " 'Well, the old boy was no St. Anthony in his day. And even now—women go nuts over him. All the women painters are wild to paint his picture. And every sculptress wants to model his head' " (*All I Could Never Be*, p. 85).

Even beyond "blind hero-worship," Yezierska says that she increasingly saw Dewey as a god. "I thought if ever God was visible in a human face it was here, in him" (*Red Ribbon on a White Horse*, p. 112). "She had sought escape from what she was. Therein lay her weakness. . . . Abandoning the God of her fathers. Setting him up as her new god" (*All I Could Never Be*, p. 203).

In *Red Ribbon* and *All I Could Never Be* are two exactly parallel accounts of a near-final climactic scene between the Dewey and Yezierska figures; she shows each time that her own desire to make him more godlike than human leads to a confrontation and break between them.

In the account in *Red Ribbon on a White Horse*, she walks with John Morrow, who "was more my own than my mother and father."

Instinctively, as if he read my thoughts, he took my hand in his, caressing the palm. He interlocked his fingers with mine. And so we walked till we found ourselves at the pier under Williamsburg Bridge. Behind us were the black silhouettes of factories and tenements. Before us the deep, dark river. The current seemed to pull us down into its drowning depths.

"I never learned to swim," I said. "The river fills me with terror." "Don't be afraid," he whispered.

For a long moment we stood silent. Then I was in his arms and he was kissing me. His hand touched my breast. The natural delight of his touch was checked by a wild alarm that stiffened me with fear. I had the same fear of drowning in his arms that I had of drowning in the river. His overwhelming nearness, the tense body closing in on me was pushing us apart instead of fusing us. A dark river of distrust rose between us. I had not dreamed that God could become flesh. . . .

Old fears bred into me before I was born, taboos older than my father's memory, conflicts between the things I had learned and those I could not forget held me rigid (p. 113).

In *All I Could Never Be,* Fanya Ivanowna explains her resistance: "Each, in his separate orbit, had traveled centuries to reach that moment. He had left the track of generations of puritan training and burst into this blaze of life. And she, who had longed for the warm intimacy of that other race that had always been locked to her—she, in her blindness, had resisted that which she had roused in him—resisted not only him but herself" (p. 102).

In both versions of this episode, the female character almost immediately regrets resisting the man's embrace,[55] but when she tries to talk to him about it the next day, he is remote, "his

---

55. Louise Henriksen's analysis of her mother's seeing Dewey as father, Pygmalion, god, underlies her own perception of Yezierska's reaction: "In a sense, though she was flirting with him, she was hiding this fact from herself because, though she desired the consummation, it was also to her as unthinkable as incest (with her father), irreverence (to desire God), and plain adultery (a married man).

"Dewey had a right to expect, from Anzia's volatile, emotionally direct temperament, her seeming honesty (and the fact that she was not 23 but 33, married and a mother as well), that she would virtually burst into flame at a touch. It was he who had always been reserved, disciplined, unwilling or afraid to act on emotional impulse. He discovered like a harsh blow that Anzia had been playing a role. . . . In other words, she was emotionally an adolescent."—Henriksen to Boydston, 9 July 1975.

face a mask, his voice a monotone" (*All I Could Never Be*, p. 102).

His eyelids dropped, and his face, undefended by his eyes, lay open to my gaze. I was appalled at its sadness.

"You have a great capacity for unhappiness," he said.

"My unhappiness is only loving you."

Harsh lines rose between his brows. "You want love, but you do not want me. You do not love me. You only dramatize your want of love—"

His eyes softened, and he bent toward me. "Some day when you're older, you'll see I have nothing more to give you. I've given you everything I had" (*Red Ribbon on a White Horse*, pp. 115–16).

Louise Henriksen, Yezierska's daughter, has suggested that if this scene accurately reflects what happened between John Dewey and her mother, "maybe he was also disappointed in himself as much as in her, when the magic ended." In much the same spirit, Yezierska herself wrote, "Dimly, very dimly she glimpsed the disappointment, the disillusion drowned in his [work]" (*All I Could Never Be*, p. 103). In both novels, Yezierska attributes a break between them to the kind of scene quoted here in detail. She does, however, in "Wild Winter Love," offer an alternate version: after the novelist Ruth Raefsky has been left by her lover and has committed suicide, her relatives and her friends are discussing the tragedy. One of them says, "Well, what can you expect? Left her husband, her child, for an affair with a married man," and another adds, "You can't blame the man. The wife and daughters got wind of the affair. He couldn't let them be hurt. Why should his innocent family suffer?" (p. 491). This version has the typical Yezierska nuggets of fact: she herself had left her husband, not for another man but because she found the domestic scene stultifying; she fled with her infant daughter to California at least two years before she met John Dewey. In less than a year, finding that she could not support herself and her child there, in 1916 she sent her daughter back to her husband and his mother in New York, where Louise Levitas grew up. When Yezierska returned to New York, she lived alone, working at her writing.

Despite her several efforts to reestablish a relationship with Dewey that she describes in *All I Could Never Be* and *Red Ribbon*, Yezierska's fictional accounts agree that she was never successful. In her review of *Democracy and Education*, what might have seemed in 1921 to be an acid public comment about Dewey seems today to be an open plea to him not to "choke the feelings in his own heart":

Can it be that this giant of the intellect—this pioneer in the realms of philosophy has so suppressed the personal life in himself that his book is devoid of the intimate, self-revealing touches that make writing human? Can it be that Professor Dewey, for all his large social vision, has so choked the feelings in his own heart that he has killed in himself the power to reach the masses of people who think with the heart rather than with the head? [56]

Whatever happened to estrange Dewey and Yezierska, she was, she said in *All I Could Never Be*, "miserably and humiliatingly in love with this man who no longer loved her. The shame and the hurt of it would go on gnawing and burning to the end of her days" (p. 110). Her writings, particularly the last two novels—published fifteen and thirty-three years after Dewey and Yezierska met—offer convincing testimony of her continuing feeling for him.

The impact on Dewey of his relationship with Yezierska, although largely expressed in the poems discussed at length earlier, is apparent in a number of others. In only one poem, however, a poem also possibly inspired by Yezierska—purposely and appropriately entitled *Swinburnian*—does Dewey's sensuous poetic enjoyment of nature verge on sensuality. Markedly different in tone from the other love poems, this seems to be an experiment in direct imitation: taking Swinburne's *Dolores* as a point of comparison, the parallel expressions are too similar to have been accidental.[57] For example, Dewey's "scorpion stings of devils' whips" that "Were as of old thy lips upon my lips," had appeared in Swinburne's lines, "On thy mouth though the kisses are bloody, / Though they sting till it shudder and smart," and "By the pleasure that winces and stings." As Dewey wrote of dreaming in the surf of a sulphurous sea until the "irregular restless flames of hell" rose and fell, "And their sharp stings were kisses of thy breath / As in the days thou kisst me unto death," so Swinburne had written, "As our kisses relax and redouble / From the lips and the foam and the fangs," and

---

56. "Prophets of Democracy," p. 496.
57. *The Works of Algernon Charles Swinburne: Poems* (Philadelphia: David McKay, 1910), p. 66.

xlvii

> The froth of the serpents of pleasure,
> More salt than the foam of the sea,
> Now felt as a flame, now at leisure.

Swinburne described how "the fume of thine incense abounded, / To sweeten the sin," which Dewey's *Swinburnian* echoes as "While the foggy smoke of the smoth'ring fumes / Were as the delicacies of thy perfumes." Even the repeated 's' alliteration, which is most effective in his re-creation of the soft surf in which he "dreamed, surgent, resurgent," is also noticeable in *Dolores* in such lines as "On sands by the storm never shaken," and "Thy skin changes country and color, / And shrivels or swells to a snake's."

The evocations of physical response that suffuse *Swinburnian* are not widely characteristic of other poems in the personal group; aside from passing references in *Two Weeks* and "There stirred within me" to the surging of blood and the "touch of hands that did enhance / Desire till distance lost its stern avail," only three other poems make extensive reference to physical sensation. As Dewey wrote in the poem that appears as an epigraph to this volume, each poet's experience, even though expressed in lines that "repeat what's old and worn," may reveal both "fresh joys" and "the woes of fresh made hells." One of his "hells" was the pain concentratedly revealed in *Romance, My Fever,* and "Across the white of my mind's map." In *Romance,* which may, like *The Round of Passion,* be an extended metaphor of a love relationship, the poet experiences an imaginative flight "In the suave caressing air," with minute description of physical sensation. But when "Down he fell / To where he was before," all the pleasurable feelings of the flight were converted into "one void but full of / Pain and emptiness." In *My Fever,* he says,

> My body of crowding pains a vase
> Of flaming fev'rish flowers was.
> My bones not mine but a tight mesh,
> A trap, a snare, in which soul slunk
> In kettle of hot seethings shrunk,
> Where boiled and bubbled pulsing flesh.
> . . . . . . . . . . . . . . . . . . . . . . . . . . . . . . . . . . . .
> Till my body, with all else blent,
> Grew big to be the only world—
> World of reptiles that writhed and curled

> Across an universe of aches
> Boundless involved without breaks.

In the poem "Across the white of my mind's map," emotional suffering and erotic longing are blended in a delicate balance, causing pain like that of fever,

> As if the sun had drawn its belt
> Around the bulging girth
> Of my hot swollen earth
> Where desert sand waves vainly lap
> To quench a heat they but swallow
> As fire after fire doth ceaseless follow.

Another poem, *My Body and My Soul*, refers also to the body, but to make a philosophical point rather than to describe sensation or response. In 1916, Dewey wrote about the "obstruction" created by "the currency of moral ideas which split the course of activity into two opposed factors, . . . the spiritual and the physical," which he saw as a "culmination of the dualism of mind and the world, soul and body, end and means." [58] How strongly he opposed such dualism is apparent in his 1930 autobiographical statement where he remembers that early in his life, "divisions by way of isolation of self from the world, of soul from body, of nature from God, brought a painful oppression—or, rather, they were an inward laceration." [59] This concern is the theme of *My Body and My Soul*, where he emphasizes that neither strictly "physical" nor "spiritual" love is possible.

> Those church-hung bells an empty foolish chime do toll
> Droning: One love from body is, another love from soul.

Trying thus to divide love into two kinds is wrong,

> For love is proved in power to wait in worship, serve and
> give,
> And soul without body, powerless for these things, does not
> live,
> But pretentious ghost, filled with thoughts of self, wanders
> alone

58. Dewey, *Democracy and Education* (New York: Macmillan Co., 1916), p. 402.
59. Dewey, "From Absolutism to Experimentalism," p. 19.

> While body's love, in glad surrender, finds other's soul his
> own.

In contrast with his poems about the "fresh made hells" of pain, many of Dewey's personal revelations have the optimistic tone of the "fresh joys" that he says in the epigraph to this volume his poetic lines might disclose. He asks in No. 67,

> Because the plan of world is dim and blurred
> Not some wise God's clear utter'd word,
> Shall I resentful stand in scorn
> Or crushed live dumb in mood forlorn?

And his answer is a forceful "no," not

> Till loving friendships pass and fail;
> Till wintry winds do lose their glee
> And singing birds no more are free.

Despite occasional mentions of frailty, such as in No. 28, where he says he was "Too weak / To bide the consummation of his dreams," or in *Little Things*, where he describes himself as "a feeble thing," he declares in No. 41 his innate confidence that if his "frail ship" loaded with "limitless freight / Of hopes and loves" can

> harbor win in victory
> 'Twere a marble bridge spanned across the sky
> Over which hereafter surefooted caravansery
> Should constant pass and wondrous traffic ply.

Underlying Dewey's gentle demeanor and modest manner was a deep core of self-knowledge and self-confidence, which is apparent in poems such as *My Road*, where he says,

> Adown the mottled slopes of night
> With smile that lit the dark,
> Ran a little lane of light
> That none but I could mark.

Writing these poems in the years of his fifties, Dewey apparently already considered himself as "aging," if not actually "old." This aspect of his self-image seems curiously premature today in light of our knowledge that he had some forty more years to live. But even his frequent references to his aging are characterized more by acceptance than by frustration or rebellion. The most lighthearted of these is in *Time Laid Low*, where

1

"love's little bow" is the weapon that "lays time low." As he says in "Not wrinkled, shrivelled, grey,"

> I too have turned the road's long day,
> And have not found that age 's mere blear
> And blot and bunchèd pains, and fray
> Of worn out garb.

Similarly, he declares in *Two Births*, "Tho life's fire of kindled rage divine / Long since burnt low, I bear no grudge." In *Two Weeks*, he contrasts for Anzia Yezierska his own "long drawn experience / Of age" and "the host / And unnumbered diversity by which age counts" with the "passions few and deep" of the young. During this same period, he expressed in a prose note his understanding and acceptance of the effects of growing older; after commenting to Elsie Ripley Clapp that we are all limited, restricted, "bound to some extent," he adds that his view might be "only a philosophizing of age—hardening effects of age, old age. But yet, again, is not aging a constant?" [60]

Counterbalancing the general optimism and honest acceptance of reality more characteristic of the Dewey image, a number of his poems express weariness, frustration, depression, or just simple lack of feeling. Abstractly and impersonally discussing psychology, he had asked Clapp in another note, "Doesn't the moment come when energy flags to keep up the effort, the struggle, to think things through and so keep action, and the tiring shows itself in quitting the thinking—falling back on unredeemed desire?" [61] He expresses exactly the same reaction on a directly personal level in *To Conscience*,

> I have struggled and am tired
> Of this road embriared;
> Let things take their courses.

But it is not only the active struggle that from time to time overcomes Dewey; dreary routines also bring feelings of futility and frustration, as in "I wake from the long, long night," quoted earlier, "Joyless, griefless, begins the round / Of day's unillumined duties."

---

60. Dewey, " 'A' The Factual-Desirable," 10 October 1911, Clapp Papers.
61. Dewey to Clapp, 18 November 1911, Clapp Papers.

He notes in *Two Births*, "the gallant voyage of mine / Turned to an unadventurous trudge."

Whether he feels real weariness or simple suspension—as in "Long time lay the world level and open," where he says that

> No heights of hope or subsidence of woe
> Gave poignant meaning to time's unceasing flow

—nature is the most frequently sought source of peace. In "Fair flowers grow in my garden ground," he says, "Come to this slow and gracious peace. / Let striving be; let conquest go." The "slow and gracious peace" is

> where noises cease
> To stir, where quiet roses blow
> In careless beauty, without thought
> Of yesterday or morrow. How
> Shall we not rest, by nature taught!

In "Not now thy scourging rod," a plea for rest patterned directly on the Twenty-third Psalm, he says to God,

> Spare thy just avenging wrath;
> Walk with me a grassy path
> Beside still waters for a little hour.

After "pacing the cool earth," they can

> laugh
> To hear the foolish crickets sing
> And see the pent in worms take wing
> —Butterflies.

Since "Yet all too long shall be thy eternal day," he invites, "Then for a little while, come God and play."

The very writing of poetry must have been for Dewey an escape into peace; he noted approvingly in *Art as Experience* that Spenser described poetry as "the world's sweet inn from pain and wearisome turmoil" (p. 280). Suitably befitting a poetic search for tranquillity and peace, this theme is embodied in gentle, quiet imagery. Dusk, twilight, and above all, night, symbolize the longed-for quiescence, as in No. 29:

> Tho't was lost
> In the endless reaches of the night
> Whose welcome peace repaid the cost

Of the struggles the driving light
Had roused.

In *A Moment and a Time,* "night distilled her dew / To yield a shining gift to day's glad blue." Night is also seen as "mystic mother" and "mother soul," in No. 60:

Now night, mother soul, broods the weary hours,
Flutt'ring fugitives from the tasks of day,
. . . . . . . . . . . . . . . . . . . . . . . . . . . . . . . . . . . . . . . . . . . . . .
All embracing night,
Mystic mother, in her patience endless
And unconquerable, makes them her own,
As within death's majestic solitude
Blend the struggling spirits of severed men.

This figure, comparing night with death to describe the peace brought by both, also appears in the poems that specifically treat death. A notable exception, however, is *But,* which echoes the theme of the futility of life found in the poems reflecting weariness and tedium. With uncharacteristic cynicism, he closes this poem with the lines,

Nor is it life nor is it death
This dying life of ours
But idle blowing of a breath
That fills and sucks the hours.

In *Life,* death is seen as "a sleep— / End of desire." In contrast with *At the Last,* where he faces death with "icy passion drear," "forgetfulness"—the mother of sleep and death—is welcomed in No. 73 as "Thought's peaceful sepulcher," and "Mind's final bride." *To Death* addresses death as "my love," and says,

To me the silence comes
As I pass within thy spacious night
To more than rest, at one with thee.

Dewey's treatment of death in *Two Births* is the clearest reflection of his complete identification with Nature:

No thief is nature but mother
Whose power shall not lack
To turn me in time to clean brother
Worm and sister flower and laden air

liii

> To feed the tender sprouting plants
> Till in their mingled life I share
> And in new measures tread creation's dance.

The second general category of poems in the collection comprises those more impersonal ones in the philosophical group. The chief themes in these poems are: nature, from the cosmic to the close-by; intelligence; desire; the search for truth and for the good; social problems, man's struggles, and man's courage.

Dewey's statement about nature in *Art as Experience* aptly describes his quasi-Emersonian approach to nature in these poems: "Nature signifies nothing less than the whole complex of the results of the interaction of man, with his memories and hopes, understanding and desire, with that world to which one-sided philosophy confines 'nature' " (p. 152). This view is especially well illustrated by *Creation,* by far the most important poem in this group and, probably, in the whole collection. Dewey surely considered this a substantive, significant philosophical statement; he obviously worked on it at various times and in varying ways. Only *Two Weeks,* written for expressly personal reasons, is longer; by comparison, *Creation* is much more carefully constructed, with five complete sections and clear stanza divisions. One of the only two poems with a complete original and carbon copy, *Creation* also derives added importance from the existence of several variant versions of its material.

*Creation* moves from a picture of pre-creation, when nothing existed but "sterile Time," through the beginning of life activity and of physical ordering, into human history that is at first indiscriminate, "careless of offspring come and gone," and, finally, to the emergence of morality and of human sensitivity to value priorities, when "Time was won to love of feeble things that die, / And turned to tender care of all that grows."

Writing about the impact on his own thought of T. H. Huxley's *Elements of Physiology* [62] when he studied it in college, Dewey said, "Subconsciously, at least, I was led to desire a world and a life that would have the same properties as had the human organism in the picture of it derived from Huxley's

---

62. Thomas Henry Huxley and William Jay Youmans, *The Elements of Physiology and Hygiene* (New York: D. Appleton and Co., 1868).

liv

treatment." [63] He continued to read Huxley, whose 1893 Romanes Lecture, "Evolution and Ethics," undoubtedly inspired *Creation.* [64] This composition is also Dewey's precise early rendition in poetry of an insight expressed years later in the prose of *A Common Faith,* where he said, "Natural piety is not of necessity either a fatalistic acquiescence in natural happenings or a romantic idealization of the world. It may rest upon a just sense of nature as the whole of which we are parts, while it also recognizes that we are parts that are marked by intelligence and purpose, having the capacity to strive by their aid to bring conditions into greater consonance with what is humanly desirable." [65] *Creation* is Dewey's statement of what Sidney Hook calls the "cosmic piety" that "is possible without sentimental glorification of nature, or acquiescence in every brute fact just because it is so." [66]

Whether Dewey is depicting nature on a cosmic symbolic level as in *Creation,* or as a close-by beloved environment in *Indian Summer at the Farm,* or whether he is using nature images in connection with other themes, two figures predominate: dusk and the horizon. His preoccupation with both was still apparent in 1934 in *Art as Experience.* First, on "horizon," Dewey quoted Tennyson's lines from "Ulysses":

> Experience is an arch wherethro'
> Gleams that untravell'd world, whose margin fades
> Forever and forever when I move.

And he added, "For although there is a bounding horizon, it moves as we move" (p. 193). In his poems, this attraction of

63. "From Absolutism to Experimentalism," p. 13. Dewey's own copy of Huxley's *Evolution and Ethics* (New York: D. Appleton and Co., 1894) in the John Dewey Papers, Southern Illinois University at Carbondale, is heavily annotated and underlined.

64. On the evidence that Alice Dewey's comments on the original of *Creation* were written after 1906, it can be hypothesized that Dewey was moved in 1911 or 1912 by the work of Henri Bergson to re-read or reconsider *Evolution and Ethics.* In one of the two items he published in 1912 on Bergson, Dewey asks rhetorically, "Who to-day is not reading Bergson[?]" "Perception and Organic Action," *Journal of Philosophy, Psychology and Scientific Methods* 9 (1912): 645.

65. Dewey, *A Common Faith* (New Haven: Yale University Press, 1934), p. 25.

66. Sidney Hook, "Portrait: John Dewey," *American Scholar* 17 (1947–48): 110.

the horizon image is already apparent; he responds to it descriptively at times, at times figuratively, and some of his fascination with it can be seen in these examples: *Mine Own Body*, "Beyond the sloping earth's far rind"; "Generations," "Beholding the horizons / Tremulous with the generations / Of the dawn"; *Natural Magic*, "Luminous mists by the dim edge / Of earth's horizon"; *But*, "By the domed sky's far rim"; No. 49, " 'Gainst where heav'n and earth together grow"; and No. 52, "Yonder where the horizon clears / Its farthest rim."

About the other predominant nature image—dusk—Dewey said in *Art as Experience*, "At twilight, dusk is a delightful quality of the whole world. It is its appropriate manifestation" (p. 194). In his poems, too, he sees "dusk" (or "twilight") as the "appropriate manifestation" of the world. In "Last night I stood upon the hill," he says that

> Dusk, in waves and huge oceans,
> Poured from some God's forgiving source
> And blotted up each darting ray
> With which the fierce divisive sun
> Sought to sustain the stir and sway
> Of the unrest with which he had begun
> The break of day.

Sometimes he uses "twilight" and sometimes "dusk": in "there stirred within me," he mentions the "tender twilight creeping to the sky's last ray"; in No. 60, "As stole twilight, / Humble herald of unwingèd vict'ry"; and in No. 24, "The dusks thy ling'ring beauties seem." Dusk is a time of pause and promise in *A Moment and a Time*, when

> The swift feet of day were captured
> In twilight's interwoven hedge.

In the same poem, he refers to "dusk's capacious room," and in *Indian Summer at the Farm*, to

> Vine flowers at night-fall—
> Of light and mingled dark
> Creeping up dusk's high wall.

*A Peripatetic's Prayer* is, like *Creation*, a significant poetic-philosophical effort, and is the only other poem in the collection which has—along with a complete draft variant of the second page—carbon copies corrected like the original. This poem illustrates a major theme in the philosophical group: the importance of human intelligence, mind, knowledge, wisdom. Here, the "cycling generations" are attracted "To their final end, intelligence," a process not disturbed by "Things that changing wane and wax, / For lack of Mind, their true essence." "Knowledge of knowledge" is the "supremest good" and Dewey's "prayer" is: "By love of learning let me find / My own last essence, Mind." Similarly, he wrote:

> My mind is but a gutt'ring candle dip
> With flick'ring beams the wind doth blow around;
> Yet the scant space thus lit is holier ground
> Than that where prophet did his sandal slip
> In token of the presence of his Lord.

However, insistence on the intimate relations between the power of intelligence and "warm emotion" is a common Deweyan theme. As he said in his *Human Nature and Conduct* chapter on "Desire and Intelligence,"

The separation of warm emotion and cool intelligence is the great moral tragedy. This division is perpetuated by those who deprecate science and foresight in behalf of affection as it is by those who in the name of an idol labeled reason would quench passion. The intellect is always inspired by some impulse.[67]

In his poetry, too, the influence of emotion—particularly desire—on intelligence is a clear theme. Also in *Human Nature and Conduct*, Dewey said, "Desire is the forward urge of living creatures" (p. 249), and "Some moralists have deplored the influence of desire" (p. 194). He states the same two concepts poetically: in *Borrowed*, "Desire . . . drives its ship the soul," and in *Duplicity*, when Desire sends men "to the lovely rose . . . / In warning speaks the stern-lipped moralist / Of beauty's lure to hidd'n thorn and briar."

Dewey said that even though the "moralists" found "the heart of strife between good and evil in the conflict of desire with reason, . . . reasonableness is in fact a quality of an effective relationship among desires rather than a thing opposed to desire," and, in the same vein, "rationality . . . is the attainment of a working harmony among diverse desires"

67. Dewey, *Human Nature and Conduct* (New York: Henry Holt and Co., 1922), p. 258.

(*Human Nature and Conduct*, pp. 194, 196). This same view is expressed in his poem "Two extremes of one joinèd theme," where the "joinèd theme" is Desire. As he said (*Human Nature and Conduct*, p. 258), "Even the most case-hardened scientific specialist, the most abstract philosopher, is moved by some passion," so he also urges poetically,

> Let mortals from earth on passion's wings aspire
> Rising by love and lust to reach the godlike mood
> Of men raised high beyond all that's higher
> Like gods enjoying their heart's Desire.

That goal is the "poet's vision, darling dream, / Lovelit home of heaven for mortals." The opposite extreme is

> preachment of sin's punishment in mire
> For souls sucked beyond hell's portals
> By dev'lish trafficker in men, their buyer
> By lying promise of fulfilled Desire.

In 1932, Dewey wrote that the "task of moral theory is . . . to frame a theory of Good as the end or objective of desire, and also to frame a theory of the true, as distinct from the specious, good." [68] The search for this "true good," and especially the continuing, never-ending need for that search, is treated in several poems. It appears in capsule form in *Truth's Torch*:

> Heed not the lies
> In idleness conceivèd
> Of truth's illumined skies
> For aye and aye retrievèd.

> No course is lit
> By light that former burned
> From darkness bit by bit
> The present road is learned.

He sounds in No. 75 a similar warning against building on "retrieved truth":

> By power of words gone things revive;
> To live in some awful potency

68. Dewey and James H. Tufts, *Ethics* (New York: Henry Holt and Co., 1932), p. 205.

> Like gods that decay of death survive;
> . . . Till man's present life in past may root.

This dangerous "power of words" is characterized in the same poem as "Language, fourth dimension of the mind, / Wherein to round square things are curled."

Dewey admonishes those who "yet repining grieve / That truth should follow changing ways" (No. 89), and in two closely related metaphors, reminds all seekers after truth that they must rely on their own resources in this perilous search. *Truth's Torch* says,

> Never to thy searching sight
> Does the true road appear
>
> Till dart th'arrows
> Of thine own lifted flame
> Through clinging fogs that close
> And hide the journey's aim.

And *Unfaith* says that "the things you claim to greet" must be "known by you from light of inner soul / —Light flaming from your own life's self-mined coal—."

In his search for the good, man's desire for certainty can tempt him to try to distinguish "fixt ill" from "fixèd good," which is the theme of *Paradise Lost and Regained*. Dewey says that " 'Twas a devil subtly wise" who beguiled the human race with the idea that such distinctions are possible, because "Well he knew thus dividing good from ill / Discord should keep the rule of human will." The only way man will find "liberation from illusion's veil" is simply by choosing between better and worse, because

> When chosen is the better from the worse
> 'Mid mingled flowing good and ill
> A new created God dispels the curse;
> And from the doubled mixture grows a single will
> That this world which subtly mingled is
> Shall ever better come to be, till man knows
> That such growth of better is his sole bliss.

Also in *Paradise Lost* appears a striking parallel with Dewey's familiar lines in *Reconstruction in Philosophy*: "Let us perfect ourselves within, and in due season changes in society will come of themselves is the teaching. And while saints are

engaged in introspection, burly sinners run the world." [69] In
*Paradise Lost,* the "subtly wise" devil knew that

> by placing good beyond the far sky
> Where it may not be reached—for 'tis so high—
> Th'earth below should stay a pleasant seeming hell
> Where he and his friends might prosperous dwell.

The direct as well as allusive references to the Bible sprin-
kled throughout the poems are a reminder of Dewey's early
religious training and of his "higher criticism" approach to the
Bible in church-school classes he taught while at the Univer-
sity of Michigan. The poem patterned on the Twenty-third
Psalm ("Not now thy scourging rod") has been mentioned, as
has his allusion to Moses in No. 34, "where prophet did his
sandal slip / In token of the presence of his Lord." Other ex-
amples appear in *Two Births,* which mentions the "wonder
food / Miraculous more than that the raven / Brought Elijah,
God's nested brood"; *Paradise Lost* refers to the devil's having
caused man to be shut out from paradise by tempting him
with "fruit of that forbidden tree"; in *Little Things,* addressing
God, he says, "thy Son / Hath said 'What is last, first shall
be' "; and in "Rough mountains once were freedom's home,"
appear the expressions, "all things will be given to you,"
"take no care for the morrow," and "the dying sacrifice of th'
loving Lord."

Direct religious expressions, however, are a mixture of con-
ventional poetic invocations of the Deity, of deeply humanistic
sentiment, and of anti-theological comments. Although his
published prose during the 1910–20 decade is not marked as is
*A Common Faith* by explications of his concept of "God," he
did not shy away from using the term, and in varying ways, as
he uses it also in the poetry. For example, in a 1911 note to
Elsie Ripley Clapp, he defines God as "the particular form that
thinks—knows—acknowledges, all other forms." [70] Also in
1911, in another unpublished note, he draws the analogy
"law, the state, God: the umpire, judge, harmonizer." [71] The
paucity of such references in printed materials is probably

---

69. Dewey, *Reconstruction in Philosophy* (New York: Henry Holt and Co.,
1920), p. 196.
70. Dewey to Clapp, 21 October 1911, p. 3, Clapp Papers.
71. Dewey, "Time 1," 14(?) November 1911, Clapp Papers.

explained by Dewey's statement to Herbert Schneider in 1929;
when Schneider asked him when he "got over Coleridge [the
*Aids to Reflection*]," Dewey responded that he never had:
"Coleridge represents pretty much my religious views still,
but I quit talking about them because nobody else is inter-
ested in them." [72] He also offers a simple explanation for the
complexity of these kinds of references in the poetry. In *Hu-
man Nature and Conduct,* he writes: "Man is not logical and his
intellectual history is a record of mental reserves and compro-
mises. He hangs on to what he can in his old beliefs even
when he is compelled to surrender their logical basis" (p. 224).
Thus in Dewey's poetry, references to God range from the
identification of God with nature in *Two Births,* which calls
"the world, our God," to the implicitly anthropomorphic fa-
ther figure of "To us you came from out of dark," where the
dead child is "God's own loan," and of *One Night,* in which

> God walked the earth
> God walked the sky
> To seek delights for you.

But in addition to these references and those quoted from *Par-
adise Lost,* Dewey speaks of God and religion somewhat ironi-
cally: in No. 67, he says, "the plan of world is dim and blurred
/ Not some wise God's clear utter'd word"; in *Paradise Lost and
Regained,* "A new created God dispels the curse"; in *Unfaith,*
the Bible was "Anciently writ by those who walked with God /
(When as yet the unusèd paths he trod)"; in *My Body and My
Soul,* "those church-hung bells an empty foolish chime do
toll"; and in "Language, fourth dimension of the mind," he
writes about the "thoughts bequeathed / By mutt'ring priests"
who "spelled night ridden salvage, / From stew of time." The
poem that seems to be the most personal kind of religious
statement is *Unfaith,* a message of reassurance to "you who do
not now believe / The things you learned in childhood days,"
and who are still

> Grieving not for yourselves who endowed
> With the mind's ideal have left the crowd,
> But for those who . . .
> Still need guidance by faith's inspirèd scroll.

72. Lamont, *Dialogue on John Dewey,* p. 16.

He tells them that if they had truly learned from

> —Light flaming from your own life's self-mined coal—
> You would also know that others too with feet
> Unbound, springing like flowers from unfrozen sod,
> Would make their own way to their souls' own God.

Several poems address themselves directly to social questions—treatment of miners, need for international co-operation, pedantry and other problems related to education. The first line of No. 83, for example, introduces the theme: "Rough mountains once were freedom's home"; but Dewey says, now

> Pennsylvania's hills are tortured with mines
> Of coal and iron mid whose galleried gloom
> Men's misshapen shadows are ghostly signs
> That mountains, like cities, have sealèd freedom's doom.

The thoughts and words of "their employer" as he talks about the miners are an exact poetic rendition of a prose statement Dewey made in a set of 1911 class notes: "We do not conceive the business of the masses as a condition of *our* living well. We tell ourselves that it is good for *them*; work keeps them from evil; disciplines them; forms useful habits. With leisure they would go to saloons—easily proved since they now go to them. Carries over to working men the general theological relation of work, probation, in this world to happiness in the next—but some uncertainty as to the where and when of heaven for the present masses." [73] "Tho some of the pretty blushing ladies were shocked," is a brief companion piece to No. 83, pointing to the possibilities for development if the "black and sooty boy" could only learn to "read and write and cipher," instead of spending his youth in the "sepulcher" of the mines.

In another poem expressing sympathy for the oppressed, "Through windy gorges of the clouds," Dewey uses the metaphor of "sheep" to deplore especially the plight of those who "travelled free / Of blows, since they never thought." On the other hand, there might be hope for the rebellious ones

> who felt the lash
> 'Cross their defenceless backs
> Till woke the flame from out the ash

73. Dewey, class notes for 21 October 1911, Clapp Papers.

> other worlds awake
> From sleep of habit to the pain
> Of search and thought to keep
> Each its own true path.

This poem and the others quoted here add little factual information to our knowledge of Dewey's philosophical positions that are already set forth in his extensive prose writings. But comparison of identical ideas stated in his prose and in his poetry expands our understanding of Dewey the man both dimensionally and directionally: the poems effectively illuminate an emotive aspect in his intellectual life often not manifest in the prose, and, together, the poems in both groups reveal the broad compass and sensitive depth of Dewey's emotions, from his most intense personal feelings to his profoundest philosophical beliefs.

This overview of the major themes and some of the most typical images in Dewey's poetry can do little more than highlight the general character and quality of the poems. For clearest insights into that character and quality, one must turn to the poems themselves, because these poems, as is the nature of all poetry, are most revealing in their particularity. In writing about poetry, Dewey himself sounded in *Art as Experience* an appropriate note to end this commentary. He said that even though one can indicate and describe the subject of a work of art, "the actual substance . . . *is* the art object itself. . . . One can tell another in words the subject of the 'Ancient Mariner.' But to convey to him its substance one would have to expose him to the poem and let the latter have its way with him" (p. 110).

# 1

## Lyric Poems

## 1. Autumn

Fair is my love in body's grace
And fair and white in soul is she
Like the white wonder that lights up space
When sudden blooms th'apple tree
5      That yields itself acquist.

Yet not spring's perilous daughter she
But child of fall, dear time of year
When earth's fair fruits perfectèd be;—
Gold of grain and grapes' purpling tear
10      Of pendant amethyst.

Had not rich fall her ripe fruit brought
As proof of time's fulfillèd good
Life's inner speech I had not caught.
For how should I have understood
15      Its final meaning missed?

## 2. The Blossoming Wilderness

I dreamed a languid dream of soft deceit
Wherein lies joyous framed in counterfeit
A garden flower paved for ling'ring feet
And perfume laden through space starlit.
5  Do I but wish, lo, a path leads to gate
Opening to the broad meadows of the dawn
Where, obedient to my bidding, wait
Lions of truth and playful poesy's fawn
Near peaceful banks of joy's singing brook
10  Whose waves are as kisses to those pastures green.

And when love's pleasure garden I forsook
'Twas but to gaze upon a spread-out scene
Of lovely knowledge and lovelier art
Where they stood revealed to open view.

15  I 'woke. Gone were the lion and the hart—
Vanisht sun-lit mead, and star-lit garden too.

3

Love's garden was a stony place with weeds
Watered but by my lab'ring drops of sweat;
And if for a moment I ceased from deeds
20    'Twas as if my love and I had never met,
And across the fields of crackling thorn
I searched her out as one unknown
Since by my faithlessness I had been shorn
Of all tokens by which love doth know her own.
25    Thus sweet dream's idly drawn out fondling kiss
Awoke to love's severe attendant service.

## 3.

Empty as high heaven's heartless shell
Where sun nor moon nor stars therein do dwell;
Barren as yon salty infertile waste
Where endless waves move futile in their haste;
5    Longing like dumb and winter chillèd ground
For touch of life, warm, palpitant, flow'r crown'd;
Trembly as windswept air where light has past,
As melts the sudden snow that's askt
To nothingness by far unheeding sun—
10    The days, apart from thee, at last are done.

## 4.

Generations of stifled worlds reaching out
Through you,
Aching for utt'rance, dying on lips
That have died of hunger,
5    Hunger not to have, but to be.

Generations as yet unuttered, dumb, smothered,
Inchoate, unutterable by me and mine,
In you I see them coming to be,
Luminous, slow revolving, ordered in rhythm.

4

10 You shall not utter them; you shall be them,
And from out the pain
A great song shall fill the world.

And I from afar shall see,
As one watching sees the star
15 Rise in the waiting heavens,
And from the distance my hand shall clasp yours,
And an old world be content to go,
Beholding the horizons
Tremulous with the generations
20 Of the dawn.

## 5. Hope and Memory

Tho half my heart might keep on singing
In tune to echoed joys still ringing
Yet my hand must cease its writing
As homeless birds from plighting
5 And wounded doves from winging.

Hope's half of heart is frozen numb
Vainly waiting warmth that does not come
So mem'ry's half that still might sing,
Unable from winter to summon spring,
10 In stricken sympathy is dumb.

## 6.

I wake from the long, long night
Of thoughtless dreams, fancies
Nor pleased nor vexed. And despite
The sleep of untroubled trances
5 Joyless, griefless, begins the round
Of day's unillumined duties,
A silken web in which I'm bound.

5

Earthward my eyes, lest the beauties
Of a life not yet trammeled distract
10   My ordered paces from the path
And I no longer keep my pact
With my possessions, and the wrath
Of stern-eyed freedom break the chains
Which keep me from the wilderness of tears
15   And turn me loose to suffer in the lanes
Of thorn trees unpossessed as yet by man,
From which no harvest shall I reap
Save stabs and flames of pain, and wan
Exhaustions among th'unshepherded sheep
20   Of thoughts which travel th'untracked wild
Of untamed desire. Either this, or else I creep
To a cooped-in grave smothered by the treasure piled.
My friend your hand I ask along the lonely steep.


## 7. In Light

Heaven's one star
Beloved afar
I climbed the sky
To love on high.

5   Shy distance rent,
In splendid light
Of rapture white
Our beings blent.

No longer far,
10   But past the bar
Till time be spent
My shining star.


## 8.

Is this the end?
A past with a closing door

Thru which I hardly grasp
From out of time's jealous clasp
5    A scant fleeting store
Of memories retreating:
A future all hope defeating
Closing in with tight shut door.
Twixt the two the present penned.

10    Great God, I thee implore
A little help to lend:—
I do not ask for much,
A little space in which to move,
To reach, perchance to touch;
15    A little time in which to love;
A little hope that things which were
Again may living stir—
A future with an op'ning door:
Dear God, I ask no more
20    Than that these bonds may rend,
And leave me free as before.

## 9. My Body and My Soul

The meaning of these things I've read in books I do not
    know—
Telling of one love that high is and other that is low.
For 'tis certain that if there be love, there is but one love,
Love that goes all the way below and all the way above.

5  That I now truly love there were no way quite sure to tell
Save that, willing, love goes with me to lowest depths of
    hell,
Where, since 'tis love, 'twill lift those depths to highest
    heaven,
Beyond where dwells the great High God with archangels
    seven.

Likewise those church-hung bells an empty foolish chime
    do toll
10  Droning: One love from body is, another love from soul.

7

Only of love not from flesh and body let there be shame,
But not of love e'en that is of body halt and blind and
    maim.

For love is proved in power to wait in worship, serve and
    give,
And soul without body, powerless for these things, does
    not live,
15  But pretentious ghost, filled with thoughts of self, wanders
    alone
While body's love, in glad surrender, finds other's soul his
    own.


## 10. Natural Magic

Like the moving sea's wide liberty
Is the compulsion of the sorcery
From thy swift moving presence spread.
For ere the worlds began, thy soul was wed
5  By nature's mystic marriage pledge
To changing seasons; scents of soil;
Luminous mists by the dim edge
Of earth's horizon; to the coil
Of unsubstantial clouds brightened
10  By intangible lights of crescent moons;
To happy faery things lightened
Of all griefs; to fugitive tunes
Of dawns that fleeting winds pursue;
To gleam of wings mid red poppies;
15  To radiant worlds of dripping dew:—

To all that brightly evanescent is
Of color, sound and soft perfume
In stirring air, the waving grass,
Or ringing bells and flowers' bloom,
20  So that as you swiftly pass
Full hearts upleaping glad rejoice
As at holy incense from an altar's urn,
Or the wandering magic of voice

Of birds that together sweetly learn
25  The mingled mysteries of love
And the dear ceaseless joys thereof.

## 11. One Night

God walked the earth
God walked the sky
To seek delights for you
He sowed the stars
5  The mists he strewed
To make delights for you.

He pushed the moon across the sky
He laughed to hold the pole star firm
He led the night so dark and dear
10  With little lakes he wet the ground
Aseeking joys for you,
Aseeking joys for you.

## 12. Postponement

My heart was all unready
When that you called me so—
And now that I would go
The lights are too unsteady
5  —Grown faint and dim
In air that doth uncertain swim.

## 13. The Round of Passion

Through slow dull years
The sun did turn to wood
Barren and cold.

9

Till in sudden instant
5  The mystery of sun
(Lurked hidden in the wood)
Returned to pristine fire.
Consumed in flame
The old was young.

10  The flame soared high;
To ground th'ashes fell.
The scatt'ring winds did blow.

Gone ash and flame and wood;
Bare earth sleeps cold;
15  Sun moves remote—
All as before.
The weary way is trod.

## 14. Song

Old earth shows new with growing grass;
Green too the red-topped sorrel;
Last year's brown and bloom both do pass.
Ah, sweet, forgive, forget, and seize the moral
5  And turn to joy the yester's quarrel.

To blandness melts the chillèd sky;
In brightness buds the ash grey laurel.
The moving season draws urging nigh
To sing in voice of hymnèd choral
10  How joy may spring from former quarrel.

## 15. Swinburnian

There in the surf of that sulphurous sea
Still I dreamed, surgent, resurgent, of thee
Till th'irregular restless flames of hell
Subdued in soft unison rose and fell

10

And their sharp stings were kisses of thy breath
As in the days thou kisst me unto death,
And the scorpion stings of devils' whips
Were as of old thy lips upon my lips,
While the foggy smoke of the smoth'ring fumes
Were as the delicacies of thy perfumes
Risen from flesh of thy twinned bosom bare
And the subtle stirrings of thy scented hair.

Thus on the surf of that sulphurous sea
I swam to earth's own heaven and the glory
Of molten hours of a surrender'd past
In oneness with thy one being enclasped.

## 16.

There stirred within me
The ghosts of many a love
Some that had passed in birth,
Some that I had murdered,
And some that had feebly spent themselves
In vain yearning for the light of day.
In solemn chorus of assembled voices,
Moving with the tread of inevitable doom,
They spoke:

You shall not let our sister in
To perish in this sepulcher.
To prevent that sin
From our very graves we stir.
In resurrection from the tombs of forgetfulness
We come to bar the door.

By the sweetness of every chance caress,
By the words of love we swore,
By the quick magic of each vagrant tress,
And every sigh that from sealèd lips did pour,
By every intercepted glance
That spoke the untold tale,
By every touch of hands that did enhance

11

Desire till distance lost its stern avail,
By the drops of blood that trait'rous started
25  In warm wonder whene'er we met,
By every ling'ring kiss with which we parted,
By every sacred tear that wet
Th'innocence of our unopened scroll of love,
By every laughing joy that illumined
30  With the glow of all the stars above
That scroll when its pages opened. By all we sinned
And all we should have saved from sin,
You shall not let our sister in
To stifle in this sepulcher
35  Where from dumb death we now murmur.

For all we might have been
Eternally is she:
The surprise of the flushed welcome of the day
After th'encompassing mystery of night,
40  The tender twilight creeping to the sky's last ray,
The certain faith the new born day doth plight
To each unsullied hour that eager comes to be,
The greatness of whatever's unpossest and free
Like the glory of the unbought comradeship of earth and
    sea.

45  In her we yet shall live,
To her our unlived lives we give.


## 17. Thoughts

Glad at birth, nestled on earth,
Silk'n doves of joy—
Hover'd on high, to thee they fly
Dear Love's decoy.

## 18. Thy Mind

A pool of clear waters thy mind,
Sunlit, unrippled by any wind;
Transparent mirror of lovely things,
With depths that feed from secret springs,
Flowing from some snow capped mountain peak
Which ling'ring sun rays loving seek.

Thy faithful mind reflecting clear
All charming forms, or far or near,
Draws from that high peak its dignity,
And from those depths strange mystery.

## 19. Ties

Love's light tether
Holds all together;
'Tis gossamer—
But when it's loose
Stars slip their noose
Aimless to err.

Love's tender claim
Like trembling flame
Is never spoken;
But if we deny
Stars leave the sky
In shamèd token.

Love's tenuous bond
Frail as fern's frond
Is never seen;
But if it break
Scat'red stars forsake
Their heavenly queen.

## 20. Time Laid Low

Time with his old flail
Beat me full sore;
Till: Hold, I cried,
I'll stand no more.

5    Then heard I a wail
And looking spied
How love's little bow
Had laid time low.

## 21. Two Joys

E'en in joy remember, Sweet,
One sitting at your feet
Who joyful sends his gift of love
To you so far above.

## 22. Two Weeks

Riches, possessions hold me? Nay,
Not rightly have you guessed
The things that block the way,
Nor into what ties I've slowly grown
5    By which I am possest.
For I do not own.

Who makes, has. Such the old old law.
Owned then am I by what I felt and saw
But most by them with whom I've loved, and fought,
10   Till within me has been wrought
My power to reach, to see and understand.
Such is the tie, such the iron band.
What I am to any one is but a loan
From those who made, and own.

14

15    I have a garden of flowers and bees?
      But others built the wall and kept the flowers
      Through the long and suffocating hours
      That I might rest myself in pleasant ease.

      Yet would I have you know
20    How utterly my thoughts go
      With you to and fro
      In a ceaseless quest,
      Half annoy
      And all a blessed joy.
25    Does she now think or write or rest?
      What happens at this minute—it's just eight—
      Has she written or shall I wait
      In sweet trouble of expectancy
      For some fresh wonder yet to be?
30    Whate'er, howe'er you move or rest
      I see your body's breathing
      The curving of your breast
      And hear the warm thoughts seething.
      I watch the lovely eyes that visions hold
35    Even in the tortured tangles of the tenement
      Of a life that's free and bold.
      I feel the hand that for a brief moment
      Has been in mine, and dream that you are near
      To talk with, and that I can hear
40    Your crystalled speech
      As we converse, each to each.

      While I am within this wonder
      I am overcome as by thunder
      Of my blood that surges
45    From my cold heart to my clear head—
      So at least she said—
      Till my body sinks and merges
      In communion with the wine and bread.

      Then there's that matter of youth and age.
50    Youth's felicitous, undaunted rage
      For living against long years age has spent
      In bare existence, till there remains
      But stored up memories in detachment

15

From the things that might have been, and stains
55   Of things that should not have been and are—
The choked up fountain and th'uneffacèd scar.

Then too there is the long drawn experience
Of age. You say you have lived longer and most.
Truly, if you measure by what is deep and tense—
60   The only scale of quick youth. But if by the host
And unnumbered diversity by which age counts
Rather than passions few and deep, then not so. For each
Of the many says to every other, Renounce, renounce;
The horizon is too far to reach.
65   All things must be given up.
Driest the lips, when most full the cup.

Damn fiction, damn romance.
Since I have read, I shall never know
Whether in an ancient mirror I see prance
70   Before me mimic passions in a row,
Or if they are authentic heaven and hell.
Moreover no one can ever tell.
For we are more than simple brute
Only in that there have entered into us
75   The thoughts of others which taking root
Have bred the plant and seed whose surplus,
Saved from waste, is called ourselves.
Our own! That lie again. When one delves
One finds but the tattered shred
80   Of what one has seen, or heard, or read.
An old clothes man, a pawnbroker's shop,
A chance gathered, unwinnowed crop
Of thistles, cockleburs—and a few grains;—
Offscourings of old mountains, sweepings of new plains,
85   Romantic relics of the feudal age
Stored in today's trim realistic cage.

I told you my diet should be prose.
I did not know there would always float
Before my sight the waving lily and the beckoning rose,
90   Or that even on the city's hard paved streets
My thoughts should ever shape themselves into a boat
To bear you on every wind that blows

16

The hopes and fears that measure out the beats
Of the blood that pulses from my heart.

95  Perhaps this mixture is the better art.
You said my logic you could never grasp,
While my poetic words—thus you blessed them—
Would fall like manna on a hung'ring soul.
These words of mine make no poesy. They rasp
100 Like the harsh divisions of my mind. But invest them
With your own beauty and their final goal
Shall be more than prose. The mixture uncouth
Shall then speak to you the very truth
Of me, the broken parts of an ineffectual whole.

105 Then take me as I am,
Partly true and partly sham
Not from wilful choice
But by too ready acceptance
Of the constraining work of chance,
110 Here a blow to shape, there a luring voice
To call. If I have not wholly stood
Neither have I wholly bent.
Just th'usual mixed up mess of bad and good
I bring to you as it was sent.

## 23. The Unending Hours

I lie upon the ground,
The solid vast of air upon me prest.
The earth that bore me will not take me,
But holds me prisoned 'gainst the air.
5   I cannot live; I cannot die.

I heard her come; I did not see
I heard her move; I could not stir
And naught went free.
At last I saw and all I saw
10  —The changeless reels of change.

17

## 24. When Thou Art Gone

Thy mem'ry drives the restless brook
Thy presence haunts the forest's dream
The earth to sky repeats thy look
The dusks thy ling'ring beauties seem.


## 25.

Across the white of my mind's map
The livid equator shines like a welt
As if the sun had drawn its belt
Around the bulging girth
5  Of my hot swollen earth
Where desert sand waves vainly lap
To quench a heat they but swallow
As fire after fire doth ceaseless follow.
The mists benign, expelled my soul,
10  Fly to the frozen pole
Where rains that should have healed,
In ice are soon congealed.
Thus while the tropics fiercely burn
Migrant doves sculptured on an urn
15  Make adornment of the ashes
Forsaken e'en of fitful flashes.
So let it be till judgment day shall roll
The spread out heavens as a scroll,
And fervent heat dissolve away
20  The loins of fire and head of grey.


## 26. At the Last

Ye mete me now your measures
Dread forms to whom I lied
Frail hopes I heeled to pride
Fair loves I used for pleasures.

The maddened moment comes
Of icy passion drear
A loathsome ghost of fear
The lifetime's sins it sums.

## 27. The Child's Garden

Would God my feet might lead
To that enclosèd garden
That had innocence for warden
And hopes and dreams for seed.

5    But the freezing years did harden
And shut me in this barren field
—Docks and thistle its only yield—
And I cannot find that closèd garden.

## 28.

He failed. Though he was strong,
He was not strong enough t' await
The final word of patient fate.
He was hurried by the restless throng
5    Of feverish desires to seek
The promised land of honeyed streams
Of smooth success. Too weak
To bide the consummation of his dreams
The wilderness about him
10    Was thorny, hard to bear. His mind
Was eager, ardent for the fray. Dim
Was his closeby vision made blind
Through searchings for a bright remote
Paradise of joys. Then sudden walls
15    Closed in. The thorns were hands which smote
Him. Rocks melted. Paths were pitfalls;
The promised land swallowed in cloud.

19

29.

Last night I stood upon the hill
And gazed across the bay;
Beneath, the city drank its fill
Of night whose drug brought stay
5   And stop to those fretful motions
Wherewith man runs his futile course.

Dusk, in waves and huge oceans,
Poured from some God's forgiving source
And blotted up each darting ray
10   With which the fierce divisive sun
Sought to sustain the stir and sway
Of the unrest with which he had begun
The break of day. From earth peace rose.
From the sky it fell till all was swallowed
15   In its deep mercy. Pleasures and woes
Sank in the oblivion that followed
On the shapeless dark. Tho't was lost
In the endless reaches of the night
Whose welcome peace repaid the cost
20   Of the struggles the driving light
Had roused. Then rose the swelling moon
And gently sought its magic way
Across the waters. In a tune
Of silver'd silence merged the day
25   With night, earth with sky, the world and me.
Through the moonlight's softly shining grey
Merged rigid land and fluent sea;
By the magic of inaction beguiled
Life and death slept close reconciled.

## 30. Little Things

For I who am a feeble thing
These little things do love,
And their faint glories feebly sing—

Unlike th'exalted quire above
Of cherubim and seraphim,
Who close to throne and sceptred rod
Majestic glories loudly hymn
Of high heaven's supremest God.

Let them keep their sonorous din
For those whose minds are turned that way;
For me, let me stay housed within
This 'customed tenement of clay.
For since a feeble thing I little care
For great things greatly magnified—
And ask but breathing space of air
A plot of loamy ground, beside;

An earthen jug that creamy pours
Its welcome drink; some wheaten crusts;
A homelike hearth whence pungent soars
Grey wholesome smoke in curling gusts;
My music, the cockrel's crow at morn
To which the faithful hound replies—
All little things for angels' scorn
But my familiar paradise.

Think not, Great God, I would blaspheme
Thy great and holy name on high;
But I am wonted to this dream
Of earth, so made of stuff that's nigh
And known and loved. And since thy Son
Hath said "What is last, first shall be",
Leave me content to have begun
With little foolish things I touch and see.

## 31.

Long time lay the world level and open,
Sharing and parting a common motion
Possesst by all in wide publicity,
Meaningless thus, lacking a me and thee.

21

5    Idler than August's idle hours of dull days,
Molten to one in swoll'n heat of sun's rays,
Not divided to await approach of any ill
With shy hope and quick fear in mingled thrill,

Nor close hugging memory's menaced joys,
10    But steeped in being as bees whom honey cloys,
Passed pleasureless, painless, the even hours,
Plenitude the same as absent lack of powers.

No accent of passion's rise and fall
Spaced off the moments, marking one from all,
15    No heights of hope or subsidence of woe
Gave poignant meaning to time's unceasing flow.

## 32. Mine Own Body

Tumult and peace I strove to share
Beyond the sloping earth's far rind
Athwart the clouds, those toppling crags of air
Ravined by tooth of gnawing wind
5    As waves bite at the meek defenceless shore.

But when long uplab'ring I fetched to there,
Silent sank the harsh tumultuous roar
As it were ashes from flames' dying flare.
Gone were pale peace and riot red of life;
10    In their stead, nothingness its lordship bore.

Tumult and peace I sought at earth's old core
Where wrenched and wrackèd giants in great strife
Long wrestled. But at my approach no more
They fought, nor joined they in a festal peace,
15    But unmeaning masks all sullen wore.

Disappointed, heartsick, in trouble sore,
My o'erstrained travellings did fruitless cease.
I turned to mine own house so long forgot
And saw swinging the tutored tides of peace

22

20    That futile faring I had sought,
      While the swelling air did clamorous increase
      With summons to war's tempestuous lot.

## 33. My Fever

      My body of crowding pains a vase
      Of flaming fev'rish flowers was.
      My bones not mine but a tight mesh,
      A trap, a snare, in which soul slunk
5     In kettle of hot seethings shrunk,
      Where boiled and bubbled pulsing flesh.

      My thoughts, mixèd all with muscles, crept
      Like buzzing beetles when I slept,
      While all the foes I strove to catch
10    Wove in and out to form a thatch
      That kept me close and impotent;
      Till my body, with all else blent,
      Grew big to be the only world—
      World of reptiles that writhed and curled
15    Across an universe of aches
      Boundless involved without breaks.

## 34.

      My mind is but a gutt'ring candle dip
      With flick'ring beams the wind doth blow around;
      Yet the scant space thus lit is holier ground
      Than that where prophet did his sandal slip
5     In token of the presence of his Lord.

23

## 35. My Road

Adown the mottled slopes of night
  With smile that lit the dark,
Ran a little lane of light
  That none but I could mark.

## 36.

Not now thy scourging rod—
Thy staff, instead, oh God;—
Something to support and stay,
A guide along the ling'ring way.
5  Thy wrathful rod withhold
E'en tho my sins be infinite, untold.
Since to punish thou hast eternity,
Now for a little space let be, let be.
Spare thy just avenging wrath;
10  Walk with me a grassy path
Beside still waters for a little hour—
—Eternity thou hast to show thy power—
Lean with me upon thy staff
And, pacing the cool earth, laugh
15  To hear the foolish crickets sing
And see the pent in worms take wing
—Butterflies—unmindful of thee on high—
E'en as thou art for a little while—and I.

'Tis already known that thou art strong and I am weak
20  In all the long eternity thou canst thy justice wreak;
Then for a little while, come God and play—
Yet all too long shall be thy eternal day.

## 37.

Not wrinkled, shrivelled, grey
Goes the old and friendly year

24

But as the laden vessel may
Bewept, with sunny tear—
5   Not I shall pelt you on your way
In glad riddance of something drear
For I too have turned the road's long day,
And have not found that age 's mere blear
And blot and bunchèd pains, and fray
10  Of worn out garb. Thou'rt not so queer,
Nor is New Year so blithe and gay
As some folks foolish say.


## 38. Pulse in an Earthen Jar

It's streaked with grime
There where the potter's thumb
Left an irregular groove.
The king I suppose
5   Sits high on his throne
In a golden chamber up there.

Rags and dirt, vermin too,
This leather that was once was a shoe.
Well he was born of his mother
10  And I of mine,
And both of a long long line.
And the leather came from a grazing ox
Whose ancestors were cattle in flocks.

I wonder does *he* have time to think
15  When the one star comes out in the west?
I think he is dead;
They have smothered him.
Does he dream when the soft wind sighs
At four in the summer's morn?
20  I think he is dead.
They have choked and stifled him.

25

## 39. Respite

The shallow seas o'errun the sand
Smoking fogs the deep waters hide
A space in covert I abide
Nor wish to sail, nor care to land.

## 40. Romance

He tiptoed springily, standing still.
Stretching he teetered on his toes.
His neck stretched, his head he lifted
High, tense his breath, taut his legs.
5    He stretched, several times he stretched,
Each time more quickly, sharply raising himself.
Then he jumped.
Not jumped but started, darted,
Like a bird,
10    Clean, sharply, upward.
Above, in the air, he was about to fall.
He hung wavering, then landed.
On his shadow,
High in the air he stood,
15    On his shadow, smiling.
Again he slightly shook himself
Into a tender tremble,
And felt his grace and power.
Again he jumped,
20    Upward, this time from off
His platformed shadow, which followed him,
Upwards, followed as shadows always do.
Whenever his impulse slackened,
It caught and held him
25    In the suave caressing air.
Filling his lungs, crowing, swelling,
He sailed afield, abroad
And saw new lands with
Flames of flowers, where gay-plumaged birds

30   Flashed fire in the sun.
     Below incense bearing trees
     Fair women loved
     And brave men endured.

     Then, somehow,
35   The platformed shadow broke.
     Like a raft in stormy seas
     It parted, and through the parted pieces
     Down he fell
     To where he was before.

40   Down
     Into his wonted room; some eight by twelve
     It was, with carpet, yes and wall paper too.
     His muscles ached. Dull and sore,
     Sullen he dressed and as he dressed
45   He kicked his bed and chair,
     And swore.
     Swore stupid oaths, and squirmed to try
     Each muscle, dull, aching, sore.
     At self and shoes and shirt,
50   Composing one void but full of
     Pain and emptiness, he swore.
     About him miles of dull blur
     Stretched out into the rut worn
     Roads of Day.

## 41.

     That frail ship I load with limitless freight
     Of hopes and loves. Turning to think upon
     The pathless unruled waters, waste and wan
     Where she must adventure, or soon or late,
5    Past winds that gnaw and seas that ne'er abate,
     To find a port far beyond all that's yon,
     Where not yet even stauncher barks have gone—
     I shudder, half afraid and half elate.

For should she harbor win in victory
10    'Twere a marble bridge spanned across the sky
Over which hereafter surefooted caravansery
Should constant pass and wondrous traffic ply,
Commerce of sovereign hope and love immortal,
By evened paths to heaven's wide opened portal.

## 42.

Tho all the rhymes were long since rhymed
And in by-gone ages all songs were sung,
There are heights of joy not yet climbed,
And hearts not yet by sorrows wrung.

5    Like to bodies of babes new born
My lines repeat what's old and worn;
Yet both may bear beneath their shells
Fresh joys, and woes of fresh made hells.

## 43. To Conscience

"Arouse! Fight on! Combat and conquer;
Evil are the forces."
I have struggled and am tired
Of this road embriared;
5    Let things take their courses.

I have fought and got no gain;
Toiled and been passed by
By all save wound and pain;
Others work and take their joy;
10    Now, stern comrade, so shall I,
Sick, sick, of thy endless employ.

Shall I never know pleasure?
Never know rest from strain?
Let me sail a sea of azure

15    Wave on wave of pleasure
      Turn from treading this path of rocks
      With no drug for bruise save its stain.

      Give me rest for I am tired;
      Nor ask me how I reconcile
20    My coward's choice of pleasured ease
      With ideals that once inspired.

      Comrade conscience, cease thy talk—
      Your part but talk as mine was strife—
      While I do take this flowered walk
25    And dally with sweet soft things alluring.
      Rested mayhap, I'll resume thy hard life
      Of search, stern comrade, for things enduring.


## 44. To Death

      Art thou there, my love
      Within the pale gold silence
      In loneliness enshrined?
      Where thou waitest is my doom;
5     Move gently then within thy embroidered dark,
      Till I can send thee
      Dispatches of my love,
      Doves decked with cool bells,
      Dipping their soft wings,
10    Shining, soundless,
      In sign of my subjection.

      Endure, my love.
      The noises pass; the stir recedes.
      To me the silence comes
15    As I pass within thy spacious night,
      To more than rest, at one with thee.

29

45.

To us you came from out of dark
To take the place of him who went—
Quenched that glimmering joyous spark—
Not ours you were, but lent.

5    To us you came from out of light
Brightest of lights that ever shone
To make dark life sweet and white;
Not ours you were, but God's own loan.

With us a little while, our light, you dwelt—
10   And did we fail to care or did we care too much?
Again we saw a dying light to darkness melt
While our aching arms vainly strove to touch.
And hold our own
God's blessed loan.

## 46. Two Births

Or ere I sought the golden fleece
Seized in the fever'd clutch
Of youth, that screened caprice,
Nine months I dwelt in a dark hutch
5    Of warm and precious solitude.
Sweetly bedded in that soft haven
I fed on wonder food
Miraculous more than that the raven
Brought Elijah, God's nested brood.

10   Tho life's fire of kindled rage divine
Long since burnt low, I bear no grudge;
Nay nor that the gallant voyage of mine
Turned to an unadventurous trudge.
For as my borrowed fires burn out
15   I mind me nature used herself
To build for me a strong redoubt,
Nor think myself a stolen pelf

30

To closely guard 'gainst her attack.
No thief is nature but mother
20   Whose power shall not lack
To turn me in time to clean brother
Worm and sister flower and laden air
To feed the tender sprouting plants
Till in their mingled life I share
25   And in new measures tread creation's dance

Tho unshelter'd is the tomb
Of the rude and thoughtless clods of earth
That make my second secret womb
Yet e'en there is miracle of birth
30   And wondrous food for the mysterious life
With which the world, our God, is rife.

# 2

# Nature Poems

## 47. Creation

### I

In arid spaces as yet unsown of sun
Unsoothed by show'ring kiss of fecund rain
In blank aloofness dwelt the virgin Time.

Unchanging, garbed in pallid cloth of grey
Passive she waited through becalmèd years
Her monotonous mind wan with watching

Of which her slack sense drooped unaware.
Thus dwelt in torpid spaces sterile Time
As lusterless and lax sped noons and moons

In world that one with itself, unconscious
Moved on, unforgetting, unremembering
In apathy universal apportioned.

### II

At last came Life, unloosing his large lusts—
To ravish, host of world's unspent desires,
With breathless reek of untemper'd love of change.

Time shrank; then importunèd from within
By tremulous bidding of unknown motion
Wide spread in fearful hope her empty net.

Her grey to maddened multicolor grew
And stagnant silence teemed with groan and song,
Imaged weal and woe to be future born;

Lang'rous stars looked on, then leapt affrighted
To graze unshining spread of steely spaces,
And broke in scatter'd flames of vagrant fires,

While far fields of unfencèd bitter foam
'Whelmed placid surfaces of complacent lands
With obscene slime from th'ages upturned depths.

### III

Life captive taken in Time's rhythmic net
Learned to lead in ordered swing of measure
The slow march of stars and th'unweary'ng sun

35

That nourished unimpassioned and afar
Patient corn and sudden flame of flower
With sad sedges, dowry of untilled lands

While through wedded years of encircling law
35    Ceaseless poured the violet wine of morn
To fill th'empurpled bowl of night's repose.

### IV

But despoilèd Time in agony of joy
Felt her burdened body o'ercharged release
Loose progeny begot of outlaw sire.

40    In haste they died for they were lawless born
While Time, careless of offspring come and gone,
Eager brooded how changing births might be:—

Spangled gauds of sin, piteous tinsel show,
Wisdom gnarled in struggles whence rude it sprang,
45    Sails of truth unfurled to speed folly's ship;

Harsh screaming swords clashing brothers' armor
That black'ning blood of brothers' flesh might drip
T'enrich the waste ground whereon tyrants' thrones—

Proud marbled flowers of white with splashèd red—
50    Should rise and flourish, while whiter tombstones
Grew in moonlight appealing to the mists.

### V

Till emptied of Life's love of changing Life
Time was won to love of feeble things that die,
And turned to tender care of all that grows,

55    And in experiment of Time's changes wise,
Recovered, conscious now, eternal peace
And Eternity knew Death and Care her own.

### 48.

Dear moon and stars, and dearer yet
The woolly clouds which come and go,

And dearest thou, oh sun that blots
From view the blinded moon and stars
5    And lights the thick thin clouds
Whose playful shadows chase below.


## 49.

Earth-born dust rising in the air
Made bloom of bronze from flakes of light
Sun-shot in flame of white to where
Dancing dust motes in their upper flight
5    Paused and eager drank their earthen hearts
Full to gold'n rim of heaven sent fire.
Acquiring thus dim hazy arts
To veil hard things in soft attire
Whereby some mystic magic sense
10   Crept into the minds of men below
So that phantom things stood immense
'Gainst where heav'n and earth together grow.


## 50.

Fair flowers grow in my garden ground,
They grow in rows, some short, some tall
In beds that gravelled paths surround;
Without, a grey and ivied wall.
5    And there each day I take a stroll
And see the winged creatures dart
And quick bees suck their honied toll
From out the flow'r's empassioned heart.
The warm air hangs in a lazy swoon
10   Drunk with perfumes that lang'rous time
Distilled from magic of its daughter June.

Come to this slow and gracious peace.
Let striving be; let conquest go.

37

15

Abide Thou too where noises cease
To stir, where quiet roses blow
In careless beauty, without thought
Of yesterday or morrow. How
Shall we not rest, by nature taught!

## 51. A Fallow Field

Waving weeds of sprightly ladies
In daring mood that beck and nod
Their bonnets' plumes to some wild god
Of whom the meek till'd crop afraid is.

## 52.

From my glance backward sent recedes,
Like fields from train that onward speeds,
A fan spread stretch of dusty years,
Sand-blown of wind o'er press of deeds

5 And stir of time, till there appears
Yonder where the horizon clears
Its farthest rim, an edge of green—
Whereon dance a gay crowd of folk,
(The like of which today is not seen)

10 Upon turf trod to silky sheen
By feet which sprightly song awoke
To twinkling measures of rhythmic stroke.

The throbbing music rose and fell
All in a tranced and hushèd spell,

15 While soul of man and maiden stirred
Poignant moved by the moving word
Of love, that was, tho unspok'n, heard
Within their own hearts utter'd.
So in a lonely mountain dell

20    A bubbling spring to itself doth tell
Th' surging story of new born joys,
At sight of glad earth with green trees
Of outstretched arms, where welcome poise,
Tiptoe, expectant in the breeze,
25    Creatures breasted in down of dun
[. . .] wings flashing crimson in the sun.

## 53. In the Country

Like the voyaging of the dim uncertainties
Of a maiden's heart impelled in search
Of passionate destinies,
Tremulous the questing buds,
5    Frail with embarrassment of new beauty,
Peep from their shy withdrawn abode
In answer unacknowledged
To the wooing of the unconquered sun.

Out of the virginity of secluded winter
10    They flush with tender warmth of longing
For the mystery of full surrender
To the invitations of the single urge
That binds together the glowing ball
Of fire afar and the cool sap
15    Within veins throbbing
To burst into splendor
Of leaf and flower in unabashed embrace
Of the messengers of light and air
Who bring sure tidings of th'encircling goal of love.

## 54. Indian Summer at the Farm

Fog flowers uncurled at morn—
Wind driven in white sheets

39

O'er seas of stacked-up corn
With shooks like ships in fleets.

5    Cloud flowers falling at noon—
To red and russet trees,
Whose scattered petals strewn
Are shadows blown by breeze.

Flowers of four o'clock haze—
10   Melting impalpable
Along the garden's ways
To fields ploughed gold and dull.

Vine flowers at night-fall—
Of light and mingled dark
15   Creeping up dusk's high wall
T'enclose sleep's dreamy park.

In the long lazy hours
Of slow October days
Ever float these fleecy flowers
20   Through time's dim drifting maze.

## 55. A Journey

Virgin waters and veilèd snows
In heaven's high crystalled vault—
Foul flood that fatèd flows
To brackish seas and salt.

## 56.

Life blithe in lusty action restless and rude,
Unclouded by sombre thought of means or end,
Intent to do and make, hurrying to come, to go,
To touch, beget and leave for new begettings,
5   Unsob'red by troubled thoughts of means or end.

## 57.

Like fogs from some black cave of mournful night
Poured forth uncertain chaos its huge drifts
Of aimless space whose unverdured beaches—
Unsoothed by touch of soft and dripping rain,
5    Unfurrowed by the sun's plowshare—
Were trod but by pale Virgin Time,
Unchanging, garbed in pallid cloth of grey,
Woven of undreamed dreams, purposes unthought,
Deeds undone, unfelt fears, and dooms unboded.

10    Unawakened thru the becalmèd years
She waited, burdened with a long watching
Of which her slack sense drooped unaware,
While noons and moons sped lusterless and lax
In world that one with itself unconscious
15    Moved on, unforgetting, unremembering,
In torp'r of apathy universal.

## 58. A Moment and a Time

Close by the clouds' quick built up ledge
The swift feet of day were captured
In twilight's interwoven hedge
While the breathless world in suspense enraptured
5    Paused in an eternal moment's self-contemplation.
In the strained silence's depths of curving gloom
Human hearts arrested by the doom of nature's hesitation
Like statues stood in dusk's capacious room.
The moment passed. The moving world released
10    Sped its changing course of agitation;
The marbled stillness of eternity ceased.
In the chambered dark rose in noisy hosts
The urgent deeds of ages in their ghosts
Of troubled years and clamorous hours.
15    For new born babes eager snatched their dowers
Of deeds yet to be done, and with warm breath

41

Rescued the shrinking past from a shrunken death.
Night was thrilled as if by trumpet's flare.
As skinny worms when noon hath sunned
20  Turn to wingèd forms that light the air,
So dancing shapes rhythmic, jocund,
Gave promise of the day's resuscitation.
Again the world brooded, and night distilled her dew
To yield a shining gift to day's glad blue.

## 59. The Mountain's Hour

Deep shadowed in the dim remoteness of night's high
    tower
Close linked in unspoken spell of dark's enfolding power
In ceaseless mingling twined the moments of that wistful
    hour.

## 60.

Now night, mother soul, broods the weary hours,
Flutt'ring fugitives from the tasks of day,
Worn and wan creeping to her waiting wings.
Spread as trophies on the sun's sharp spears
5   Riven by sund'ring rays of its harsh light,
They watched in furtive fear its awful course
Till in embattled fields of streaming blood
Surrendering it sank to sullen seas
Unknown, impenetrate. As stole twilight,
10  Humble herald of unwingèd vict'ry,
Grateful they lifted their arms unpinioned
In common search of a common presence;
And groping were clasped together within
The capacious stillness of her bosom.
15  Merged in oneness of the first creation
They gather strength against the shock and strain

42

Of day's wedge-like doom of separation
Ever new enforced. All embracing night,
Mystic mother, in her patience endless
20 And unconquerable, makes them her own,
As within death's majestic solitude
Blend the struggling spirits of severed men,
While fretful time, subdued, waits in worship
Wond'ring at the enduring womb of God.


## 61. Renewal

Silent I sat in the darkness
That sinuous had crept about me.

The stiff harsh air that had stood numb
Long calloused by unceasing touch
5 Of cold indiff'rent travellers,
Sudden melted, and as sorry
For a guilt sullenly prolonged
Grew tender and tenderly caressed me.

I felt the softened air begin to move,
10 Tremulous, scarce to be perceived,
As when a mother hanging o'er her babe,
(Doubtful if it breathes so still the motion)
List'ning watches, and does not know,
E'en when sensible of slight dim stir,
15 If life she sees or hears, or feels within.

So in that hour awoke th'expectant air,
Faintly sighing, drugged from long sleep.


## 62.

The rope is cut, the anchor falls
And is left alone in the mud,
Submerged.

Oozy the slime;
5 I can feel stringy sea weeds coming,
Tangling, strangling. Rust eats.
Sinks the anchor deeper, ever deeper,
In the mud.
Not an anchor now, just stuff,
10 Part of the world's eternal waste
Some used up, some unused.
It presses hard; it hurts
The soft bosom of the sea depths,
Cruelly it presses
15 And hurts.
The yielding softness
Covers and engulfs.
No anchor now—
Waste, and oozy slime.

20 Drifts the ship. The rope end, cut,
Flaps upon the side and knocks,
Knocks. You can hear it through the blowing wind,
And through the screeching of the sails
On the masts.
25 And when I cannot hear it I know
It flaps and knocks
All the time.

# 3

# Philosophical Poems

## 63. America

Thou opened wide thy gates
And they came crowding in,
And still they hurrying come.
For they had not known rest at home,
Nor quiet nor the far and friendly solitude.
Scarcely had they stopped to wash or dress—
They came so breathless trooping in.

I know not if self-moved they came,
Or pushed unwitting from behind—
This resistless, unresisting tide
Of souls. Or were there many souls
Or one all-possessing soul
I know not. But on it flowed;
And its banners were shawls upon the head;
Its flutes the cries of babes at breast;
Its drums the pattering of the unceasing feet;
And its leader and its chieftain
Was the look on every brow intent—
The set and driving look—
Of search where man spreads friendly out
And sees the sun in kindness nod to him
Before he lays him down to die.

## 64.

And high God on his throne
Felt his throne rocking shake
Touched by man's massive moan
Making the heavens to quake.

While lower gods were driven
From off their lesser seats
By sharp piercing cries riven
Like lonesome lambs' last bleats.

47

As little babies wailed
10    Saints grew red with blame
And with white blame they paled
While babies cried their shame.


## 65.

And shall we shut the door,
Draw close the blinds and seek
The incense laden space within
Where hidden lies large store?
5    Or, staying on the stony peak
Without, shelterless, drenched,
Frailer than the storm blown birch, weak
As the flame the rain has quenched
To feebly glowing coals, shall we
10    Lift our faces to the driven sky
And in a world that's open, free,
Our faith with that of fate identify?


## 66.

And the lad eager replied: No sir, not a God damned
    Word,
But put me with the little kiddies and I shall learn
The old man's ears hearing message did burn
The old man's heart did within him yearn
5    And through the tears with which his faded eyes were
    blurred
He saw the holy spirit's dove once more descend
As it hath from the beginning and shall to th'end.

67.

Because the plan of world is dim and blurred
Not some wise God's clear utter'd word,
Shall I resentful stand in scorn
Or crushed live dumb in mood forlorn?
Or suppose there's no plan at all
But things chancèd as did befall,
Shall I frown in offish censure
Because it's all a vast adventure?

Not till I take a Stoic pose
Because ungardened grows the rose;
Not till flowers smell foul to me
And the briar rose is unfair to see.
Not while racing rivers run to sea
Bearing on their bosom this unbound me.

Wag if you wish your gloomy head
Because some man hath solemn said
"The world just happ'd by accident,
Whose good and beauty were never meant"—
But ask not me to join your wail
Till loving friendships pass and fail;
Till wintry winds do lose their glee
And singing birds no more are free.

## 68. Borrowed

Not for the sun to say,
Holding deliberation
Whether to go or stay
To seek or leave its station.

Self stirred is not the sun
Nay nor any starry world.
In grasp of alien motion
Their onward course is hurled.

49

10
The ship that moves so free
Coursing the sea at will
Knows yet no liberty:—
The winds its sails do fill.

Subtler than sun's swift trail
Desire strikes for its goal;
15
Tacking more than any sail
It drives its ship the soul.


## 69. Brave Things

Swift moving earth that gallant hung
Its lantern high on curving roof
For neighbor world to keep aloof
Warned by moon signal friendly swung.

5
Earth so gallant to dare depths of dark
Plunging through perilous spaces
With frail beam to light few paces
Ahead on time's unplotted arc.

Man, more gallant to brave th'unknown
10
With only glim'ring light from mind
To pierce a future that when shown
Is as strange room to groping blind.


## 70. But—

About the earth whereon we dwell
No gladness and no pang;
But evil magic, and a spell
To numb both kiss and fang.

5
Upon the seas no steam nor sail
To venture and to pass
But rotten hulks; lives launched to fail
Mid weeds and slimy grass.

By the domed sky's far rim, no star
10 Of memory or of hope
But a black and binding bar
Girt round bleak heaven's cope.

Out of the void no recompense
Nay nor anguisht grief
15 But slumber of sickened silence
O'er time's thin shoalèd reef.

Nor is it life nor is it death
This dying life of ours
But idle blowing of a breath
20 That fills and sucks the hours.

## 71. Duplicity

Two men arose to teach the race,
One dwelt in desert and one in garden place.
One with grave speech from deep organ mouth;
The other with lilt of lute and lyre.
5 One a harsh dry voice of drouth,
The song agleam of leaping fire;
The burden of both—Desire.

Sending her to the lovely rose
As in gladsome birth of year she freshly blows;
10 In warning speaks the stern-lipped moralist
Of beauty's lure to hidd'n thorn and briar.
Song sings of burning lips that moist have kist—
Dew-steeped petals in glow of rose afire
The burden of both, Desire.

## 72. Education

I hardly think I heard you call
Since betwixt us was the wall

51

Of sounds within, buzzings i' the ear
Roarings i' the vein so closely near,
5   That I was captured in illusion
Of outward things said clear;
And about was the confusion
Of all the grown up persons said,
More invasive than Goths and Huns,
10   Urging to this and that
Until my mind was but a seething vat.

Yet, in spite of all
Well I know I heard you call
Like whisp'ring winds of dawn
15   Those many years agone.
But said they: It is forbid
That you should hear till lid
Lifts from the things immured
I' the past; nor is it to be endured
20   That you should hear direct
Before the hull of your mind be o'erdecked
With stiff well seasoned boards
Brought from dry scholastic hoards.
And others said I must not shirk
25   My work, important work,
And when that was done, only then
Might I raise my head 'bove its pen
And for a little space
Gaze upon your shining face.

30   And tho I knew 'twas me you called,
I shrank afraid, appalled;
I thought it was not proper nor polite
For one like me to dare to claim a right
To speak with you, and to pretend
35   That you, strangely beautiful, would descend
To seek me out,
A witless lout,
And so I did always attend
To what was forced upon me,
40   Listening furtive to thy call
And desiring converse with thee
Above aught and all.

52

I knew I must speak with you then and there,
But was taught that first I must prepare
45    Properly to meet thee,
Correctly to greet thee—
And that till I was grown
I patient must postpone
The wild and free glory
50    Of frank converse with thee.
And I think they too were afraid—
My fathers and my fathers' fathers arrayed
In long receding generations,
Who with their endless preparations
55    Said, "Wait," and "Wait till you have learned,
Lest by what you seek you may be spurned."
For they knew, e'en as I now know
They ne'er should find you thus and so.

Our much preparation is a thick wall
60    Through which thy yet continued call
Arrives suppressed, altered in sense
Through medium, sound-proof, dense,
We built laborious, learning's fence,
Behind which we hide from thy creations
65    Till we change by safe translations
Wild things wondrous spoken in a tongue
Once our own, native, personal; now hung
Stammering and alien, language
Of us who labor for scant wage
70    In lands where we are foreign born
Living protected, safe,—and forlorn.

## 73. Forgetfulness

Musing on memories of things that were
Thought sank where drowse both strife and stir
In rhythmic depths of time's engulfing blur—
Forgetfulness, Thought's peaceful sepulcher.

5    Last home of things averred and things denied,
Where lapse pains slurr'd and hopes descried

53

Love's pleas soft murmured, and foes firm defied—
Forgetfulness, Mind's final bride.

Hopes' and wails', loves' and hates' vanquisher
10  Swoon of silence thy ush'ring trumpeter,
To thy outstretchèd arms all lives concur—
Forgetfulness, of Sleep and Death Mother.

## 74.

Heaven and ground, smooth sky and shore
Starry on roof, unpaved the floor
Sun smitten on earth, earth choked in sky
Sped in the circuit, live we and die.

5  Moving road without a station
Such our human habitation!—
In mists dissolve its solid walls
While wingèd time rebuilds the halls.

Fast wind and water free air and sea
10  Bound by no measure, loosed from degree
O'er a waste with no land nor ledge,
(Like foolish shore without an edge,)

Driven forever our uncaptained ship
As portless as a bobbing chip.
15  Let souls dispirited and craven
Whine for some rewarding haven,

Plumb the fathomless, weigh the anchor
Lower sails in puny rancor—
For us the salty sea, th'untamed wind:—
20  Enslaved and free, both seek their kind.

## 75.

Language, fourth dimension of the mind,
Wherein to round square things are curled;

54

Or turn unbroken inside out;
Firm certitudes melt to doubt,
5 And doubtful things, a fertile seed
Tho not existent, pregnant breed
Falsities of those who say sooth,
Lush growing i' the crops of truth—
Simples to turn Men's minds about
10 Peasant to prophet, philosopher to lout,
Making wise the humble, and sage a fool,
Stones to gods, and heaven t'earth's footstool.

By power of words gone things revive;
To live in some awful potency
15 Like gods that decay of death survive;
They haunt their former earth and sea
And sky with magic that every bruit
Of whisper'd sound echoing increases
Till man's present life in past may root
20 And men's minds today but take out leases
To use in trust the thoughts bequeathed
By mutt'ring priests who spelled night ridden salvage,
From stew of time whose kettle seethed
By poet's fancy and guess of mage.

## 76. Life

A wail, a cry,
From out the deep.
A romp, a game
Little feet that ache.
5 A spark, a flame
Ashes to make.
A toil, a name
That men acclaim
While breaths expire.
10 A moan, a sigh,
And then, a sleep—
End of desire.

## 77.

Long time the world lay level and open,
Parting and sharing a common motion,
As there it lay in wide publicity,
Meaningless lacking a me and thee.

5   Then life, with things to seek and things to shun,
Was born, frail creature that both lost and won.
And when he found, or when he searched in vain,
Dull blank things grew to meanings clear and plain;

Learning hate and love and poise in his strife
10   Through them to be himself and find his life.
Say not then our bodies are glassy shells
Behind whose walls a soul imprisoned dwells.

For 'tis the body's movement to and fro,
As loving, hating; it everywhere doth go
15   That creates a soul from soulless things,
Fairer far than that fabled soul with wings.

Then tell me not this inner soul's a screen
Through which friendship and love may ne'er be seen;
Rather is it the one clear solvent glass
20   In which all else dost show and showing pass.

Not as bars between but as the world set free
Have things thus grown to be a me and thee,
Sharing no longer an unknown motion,
Conscious swayed mingling love and repulsion.


## 78. The March

Of fraud and force fast woven
Marched the governments of man—
When each by sword was cloven
New tyrannies began
5   Of blood with tears deep mixt
Where drowned the liberties of man

As wealth and might stood fixt
To keep the severing span
That makes unequal life
10    With its undying strife
—Mortals' sund'ring ban.

Till last shared griefs awake
The slumb'ring thoughts of man
An equal life to make
15    Upon a common plan.
Now chains break; prisons yawn
Erect and forth walks man
Sunlit in freedom's dawn
For all may march in van.

## 79.

Meadows of the dawn are curtained in dusk;
Their verdure sweet a harsh and cutting stubble
Where truth lies covered with a gritty husk
Of toil and sacrifice and bootless trouble.
5    Thoughts may grow but as threat'ning spears
To pierce the flesh of him who planteth there
With nameless bodings and unassuaged fears—
Fate of him whom knowledge hath made aware.

There no beauty grows save watered by tears
10    Of babes who wonder naked at the cold,
Pruned by women possessed of travail's shears,
Digged about by men exiled from the fold
Of custom to wander in wilderness
Of savage places uninhabited.

15    But when these three meet and one another bless
The wild and wasteful world to peace is led,
And from the parched, and beaten weary earth
Burst triumphant songs of beauteous mirth.
And some have preached the dream for eternal truth,
20    And some prefer man's struggle and man's ruth.

## 80. The New World—

Of a sudden, a blazing star
Ruddier than heart of flowing gold
Swept from out the vastness of the night,
The distant, boundless eastern night.
5    As the heaven filled with strange splendor,
The world, wearied with the weight
Of its tamed courses, paused, startled
By the adventure of a soul
Whose only chart through untracked spaces
10    Was faith in the miracles courage works
Even in the timidities of custom,
And whose warmth of desire for destinies
Unimaginable had kindled that blaze of flame
Which now lit the curving heavens
15    And the spread out earth.

Whereat the world spurned its customary courses,
And half hesitant was borne by new life within
Out upon the far reaches of untrav'lled space.

And now it plunges into darkness,
20    The darkness of the unknown,
The unforeseeable, the untried.
Alone it goes. The star that shone,
Shines on and other worlds awake
From sleep of habit to the pain
25    Of search and thought to keep
Each its own true path. For the trackless
Paths of heaven are infinitely diverse,
And the stars nor meet nor cross.
Their severed searches
30    For destiny which comes to each alone,
Singular and silent,
Each in its own orbit parted,
Form the ordered constellations
Of a harmony too high
35    For the dusty things of earth
Which meet and mingle,
Which are jostled by chance winds

Foreign to the mighty solitudes
Of the heavenly places
40    Where move the strong stars,
Strong to seek and find each its own,
In that loneliness where the firmament itself
Is the only company,
And the calm eternal lights
45    The only greeting.


## 81. Paradise Lost and Regained

Now hearken and I'll relate the wile
That did the human race beguile:—
'Twas a devil subtly wise
Who shut man out from paradise,
5    Saying by fruit of that forbidden tree
We should become as far gods be
To know fixt ill from fixèd good
Where they parted stand and have forever parted stood.

Well he knew thus dividing good from ill
10    Discord should keep the rule of human will,
And by placing good beyond the far sky
Where it may not be reached—for 'tis so high—
Th'earth below should stay a pleasant seeming hell
Where he and his friends might prosperous dwell:—
15    For as this earth becomes a blessed heaven
When ferment of good doth its evil leaven,
So e'en its pleasures are sharp grief and dark woe
When man believes in other evil severed below,
And goods natural for man to enjoy
20    Grow sensual sweetness his will to cloy.

Now listening you may hear the welcome tale
Of liberation from illusion's veil:—
When chosen is the better from the worse
'Mid mingled flowing good and ill
25    A new created God dispels the curse;
And from the doubled mixture grows a single will

59

That this world which subtly mingled is
Shall ever better come to be, till man knows
That such growth of better is his sole bliss,
30   Lovelier too than lovely mystic rose
That fall of man, dividing bad from good,
Has caused to grow in its far solitude
Of Trinity, holy all its lonely days,
With but themselves alone to see and praise.

35   This tale of Good that's lost and then regained
Is shorter far than that by Milton feigned.
Long his tale, since of deed once done for all
When time was sundered from eternity's high wall.
Short this song,
40   But its practice long.

## 82. A Peripatetic's Prayer

Th'Empyrean ever whirls
Its heaven strewn of stars
Milky as lucent pearls
Close to the holy bars
5   That ward the God serene
From things of baser worth.

Thence comes the changeless sheen
Worshipped of us terrene;
Thence th'all embracing girth
10   Of its circling course impelled
To bear back th'errant cars
Of mobile Mercury, and of Mars,
Fiercely fickle from his birth,
By poise of purpose held
15   In beat to cosmic tune.

Thence keeps faithful t' th'earth
The restless fitful moon
That winds would elsewise drive
Like ballastless balloon,

60

20  In veering dip and dive
    Of gusty rise and flaw,
    To time's devouring maw
    Till e'en thin crescent dwindle
    And utterly dissolve.

25  All changes fixt revolve;
    For by Empyrean's law,
    Bound fast on form's firm spindle,
    Hard earth to thin air surges,
    While *cold* to fire doth kindle,
30  And water in earth merges.

    Intent to move in turn
    To the bright firmament
    Wand'ring elements learn
    Their appointed stations
35  Whence endless they are sent
    In cycling generations,
    That e'en the mighty Zeus
    Is impotent to loose.

    But God their unmoved mover is,
40  Who in Mind's eternal solitude
    Meditates in constant bliss
    Knowledge of knowledge, supremest good.
    Unmoved by things below h' attracts
    —To their final end, intelligence,
45  Things that changing wane and wax,
    For lack of Mind, their true essence.

    Great God and lesser gods that are
    May subtle ether bear afar
    Through all this world my prayer:
50  By love of learning let me find
    My own last essence, Mind,
    So for a little while to share
    Immortality, divine, eternal,
    Forgetting city, deed and things diurnal.

55  Then the wise master turned and talked
    With his disciples while they walked.

61

83.

Rough mountains once were freedom's home
Where winds wantoned with flags breeze-flung to liberty,
And men's unfettered steps were as the foam
That dances sunflecked on the unbound sea.
5   But Pennsylvania's hills are tortured with mines
Of coal and iron mid whose galleried gloom
Men's misshapen shadows are ghostly signs
That mountains, like cities, have sealèd freedom's doom.
There work in shifts, long nights and days,
10   Little boys of flesh and blood, like unto yours,
Driving and cursing the mules along the tedious ways
Where sullen rock the stifled fossil sun immures,
Which the miner's pick-ax carves in panels:—
More patient those men than their mules who shambled
15   Through th'earth's curious winding channels.
When work ceased, they drunk and swore and gambled;
And when they were old enough they whored
And quickly spent their hard-earned wages;
While their employer at his laden board
20   Said: "Strange it is that the devil always rages
In the souls of wicked laboring men
During the days when they are alive,
So when they die he herds them beastlike in his pen.
If they would only save, they too should thrive
25   Even as we, whom, tho unworthy, God has blest
Because we by saving have the flesh denied;
For he all things adds to them who choose the best."

And then he sighed that evil men's contumacy
Should spurn the dying sacrifice of th' loving Lord,
30   And turned to his paper that he might see
There prices of his stocks and bonds, divine reward
For his thrifty frugal check on wasteful lust,
And for his loving thoughtful care for the tomorrow.
And while the room stank with his soul's green mould and
        must,
35   Women and babes wept out their night in sorrow;
And daughters like his, sold their sacred bodies
—In what he thought surely must be pleasure—

And sodden men stilled their minds with toddies
Lest they should wake and think of soul's lost treasure.

## 84. Sorolla

And this is art!
Something
To make us jump and start;
To bring
5  New thrills to jaded nerves
And break the mind's reserves
Is art:

And yet
Surface is not to be despised.
10  Tho we forget
Solid substances alone reflect
The light with which they're deckt;—
Light so brilliant our eyes surprised
No longer search below
15  But stop with outer show!—

Yet show itself is there
To catch the idlest stare;
And since New York a place is
Where all upon the surface is
20  The City should be reminded
E'en tho by eyes that are blinded
By light
That surface may be gay and blithe;
With forms and figures lithe
25  And bright.

## 85.

Tho some of the pretty blushing ladies were shocked,
Th'eternal God is never mocked.

He took the black and sooty boy to his bosom
Where he grew a white and lily blossom;
5    For when he learned to read and write and cipher
He never bought his brothers' bones to build a sepulcher
—Whited monument of wealth dazzling to men's starved
        eyes—
Wherein to bury the trembling spirit's frail surmise.


## 86.

Through windy gorges of the clouds
The little sheep were driven,
Sometimes alone, more oft in crowds:—
To all alike no mercy given.
5    Happiest they who felt the lash
'Cross their defenceless backs
Till woke the flame from out the ash
That thickly grew in those harsh tracts
Of worn yet peopled enmity.
10   Most to be pitied was the lot
Of those who travelled free
Of blows, since they never thought;
But dreamed they should be sheep
And then be shorn
15   Till they should lighter leap
Along the pathway worn.
But from their inner peace
Heavier grew their fleece,
Till backs and bellies full
20   Of curling matted wool
Stank with their body's grease.


## 87. Truth's Torch

Think not the torch
Is one of joy and light.

Its scatter'd sparks but scorch
And die in falling night.

5    Heed not the lies
In idleness conceivèd
Of truth's illumined skies
For aye and aye retrievèd.

No course is lit
10    By light that former burned
From darkness bit by bit
The present road is learned.

Tho space shines bright
And paths are trodden clear
15    Never to thy searching sight
Does the true road appear

Till dart th'arrows
Of thine own lifted flame
Through clinging fogs that close
20    And hide the journey's aim.

## 88.

Two extremes of one joinèd theme—
Here, poet's vision, darling dream,
Lovelit home of heaven for mortals;
There, preachment of sin's punishment in mire
5    For souls sucked beyond hell's portals
By dev'lish trafficker in men, their buyer
By lying promise of fulfilled Desire.

Since yearning gods must sate their sense
On earth's off'ring of frankincense
10    Or they diminish in their high amplitude,
Let mortals from earth on passion's wings aspire
Rising by love and lust to reach the godlike mood
Of men raised high beyond all that's higher
Like gods enjoying their heart's Desire.

65

15       No wings hath passion lewd that it soar,
        But heavy weights and clogs that evermore
        Drag men down to that gloomy pit
        Where noble hopes smothered expire,
        Done to death by demons who sodden sit
20       Revealèd now in their own attire—
        Gnawing pangs of insatiate Desire.

## 89. Unfaith

       With you who do not now believe
       The things you learned in childhood days,
       And yet repining grieve
       That truth should follow changing ways:
5       Who mourn the loss of spirit's lore
       That formed the past's deep cherished store—
       Grieving not for yourselves who endowed
       With the mind's ideal have left the crowd,
       But for those who from lack of such control
10      Still need guidance by faith's inspirèd scroll,
       Anciently writ by those who walked with God
       (When as yet the unusèd paths he trod)
       With you I shall not argue—'tis not meet.

       Yet not from laughter's iron scorn
15      But that you, unknowing, still live forlorn.
       For if the things you claim to greet
       Were known by you from light of inner soul
       —Light flaming from your own life's self-mined coal—
       You would also know that others too with feet
20      Unbound, springing like flowers from unfrozen sod,
       Would make their own way to their souls' own God.

90.

While world in twain allotted united was
On labile sun's land and mock and moan of sea
Navigable seas with shores that rise and sink;
Thin marge that masted look out scarcely spies
5   [. . .] [. . . . . . .] heads with lights that wink at night
Speeding ships of sailor, host-grown guests of sea.
Loamy lands where gruelly grains grow level
To lend to man who labors, largess of bread
For mouths of little ones unlearned in labor.

# 4

# Children's Poems

91.

At night shining stars march in file
Down to the far horizon's stile
And enter into worlds unknown
Where stands, I think, God's great white throne.

5  For I have watched them disappear
And yet next night they're always here
So I think that while they are gone
They stay near him till after dawn;

Then all next day they quiet sleep,
10  Tired from climbing that long high steep;
At night again they cross earth's hem
To skies where you and I see them.

And do you think if we should dare
We too might rise to them up there
15  And pass with them to worlds unseen
Where none but you and I had been?

But father says I only dream
When this all true to me does seem.


92.

John Banding looked and said:—
"Do not weep my mother dear,
For I must go to the western land
And live as pioneer.

5  "For there the soil is rich and deep
Stretchèd out in wide prairie,
And all the winds that come and go
Bid me haste there and see.

"So mother mine weep not nor cry
10  That I should leave thy knee
Since now I am a man full grown
And cannot stay by thee."

71

"But if dear son you leave me lone,"
His mother sore distressèd cried,
15     "Who will milk the uddered kine
With stool upon their further side?

"And who will take them to the pasture
And bring them home at night?
For by the fire I sit and spin
20     Since that my body has lost its might.

"And will you leave the sheep
Both bucks and little lambs
All winter on that rocky hill
Where freeze the ewes and dams?

25     "And who will fare him to the woods
To cut up logs in pilèd cords
That fire on my hearth stone may burn
When pierce winter's winds like swords?

"And who will plow the hard hard ground
30     The grains of Indian corn to sow?
And who will yoke the dark red oxen
To bring back the crops that grow?"

"Mother dear, long have I thought,
That you should make no worry;
35     While I forth to fortune seek
Upon that far off prairie.

"For I have taken of good monies
That safe I had laid me by
And I have hired a hired man
40     To do such things when I'm not by.

"Then bide for your own sake
If you will not stay for me.
Where we have a log cabin
While there is no house or tree.

45     "And he will tend the sheep
Upon the lonely hill
He will shear their thick wool
And bring them back to kill.

72

"He will plow the stony fields
50  Where grow the maize and grain;
He will call the cattle home
And drive the creaking wain.

"He will chop the high hard trees
And fetch their logs on logging sled;
55  He will reap where he did sow
And grind the grain for bread."

"But I am old and soon shall die
And grieve by others to be buried
Not by mine own son who was begot
60  By him who long ago I loved and wed."

## 93.

Next spring earth will be all in green,
With pretty flowers on her gown;
But now she's dressed in brown
In clothes too ragg'd to be seen.

5  First comes the snow all white
To wrap her nice and warm
As rests her weary form
In sleep the long cold winter's night

Till the sun melts the snow
10  And again her sweet beauties show.

## 94. This Child's Garden of Verse

Since far spaces cannot part
Dear sister from my heart
When Janey moves to or fro
My thoughts in like motions go.

73

5      So when my heart is full of joy
       I'm sure gladness makes her employ;
       If *very* glad, 'tis a sure sign
       Her mind is joyful, just like mine.

       But when I feel quite sad and blue,
10     I know she can't tell what to do;
       Or perhaps sadness keeps her still
       While anxious thoughts her mind do fill.

       But sad or glad, I like to think
       I'm bound to her by every link
15     And while she plays and runs so free
       Tied tight to her my heart strings be.


## 95.

       I should think th'earth would be ashamed
       To wear a ragged dress like this;
       If I did so, I should be blamed
       And maybe lose my good-night kiss.

5      Nurse says that because of autumn
       The clothes of earth are old and brown;
       And if we'll wait till spring doth come
       She will put on her pretty gown

       Of green, with little sprinkled flowers.
10     Anyway it is no use to scold
       Or fret this homely world of ours—
       For she is too grown up and old.

# 5

# *Appendix Poems*

96.

Athwart the shining gleam
That seemed the sun's own light
Of joy, pierced a sharp ray,
Authentic arrow of the sun
Of truth. Dropt down and down
The veil of wilful happiness.
Through curtains of my love
Of love, I saw the calm stern love
That holds the planets to their courses.
I had tricked out a canvas sky
With lights of silly lantern stars.
Afraid of both the night and day
I moulded imitation suns
Within a darkened room.

Entered then the probings
Of the true lord of day
To pale with painful light
The sham false lights of joy
Till my soul unafraid can seek
The cool recesses of the night,
The night who is the sister of the day,
Twin child with him of earth and sun,
And kindly in its darkness
Like the very light of day.

97.

Like formless fog on aimless cruise
Over fens whence pallid waters ooze
Wand'ring I drift—

But look! Upon the leaden sky—
Whereto my thoughts, aweary, scarce may fly
A gleam, a rift—

Now to a sweet and sunlit land,
By heaven's own blue in peace o'erspanned,
I come, swift, swift—


## 98. To a Pedant

Could we peep within thy mind
'Tis sure that we should find
Store rooms clean swept and garnisht
With ornaments deckt out for show;
5      In its middle, a marble hall—
Sharp cut mosaics on its wall—
With pavèd pool long since outfished
Of any living things that grow.

In each room some cabinets
10     With pigeon-holes galore
Of fly-specked specimens of lore—
Signed and sealed evidences of debts
To stale antiquity's refurbished store;
In dining hall some cold banquets
15     Of foods saved four hundred years or more—
Relics of culture's bygone rations;
Library where all the tables
Are heaped with engraven labels,
At second-handed auctions bought,
20     Of lectures, books and annotations—
Cheap gather'd substitutes for thought—
All with sworn affidavits to allege
Such things are just that knowledge
That's fit for wise men in a college.

25     On guard, a pompous sentinel,
With garb of horn and fossil shell,
To catch, arrest and smother
Any chance idea or other
That might find its stray unbidden way
30     To those dim musty purlieus gray.

Textual Apparatus

Indexes

# Description of the Texts

## 1. General Characteristics

This description of the texts of the poems treats chiefly the physical appearance of the manuscripts and typescripts, the typewriters used by Dewey in poetry and non-poetry materials, and the evidences of authorship discernible in the documents. The content of the poems and the general recurring themes are treated in the Introduction.

Because many of the poems have no titles and are thus necessarily referred to by first lines, the convention of using quotation marks for poem titles has not been followed in prose discussions of the poetry here; instead, titles appear in italics, and first lines of untitled poems appear in quotation marks.

Six of the ninety-eight poems are completely in Dewey's handwriting; two of these—No. 12 and No. 34—seem finished, but the others have notes, jottings, and illegible phrases that indicate they might not be final products. The titles or first lines of the manuscript poems are: No. 3 "Empty as high heaven's heartless shell"; No. 12 *Postponement;* No. 34 "My mind is but a gutt'ring candle dip"; No. 74 "Heaven and ground, smooth sky and shore"; No. 90 "While world in twain allotted united was"; No. 97 "Like formless fog on aimless cruise".

The remaining ninety-two poems are typewritten. The two typed poems of which the originals are no longer in the collection—No. 96, "Athwart the shining gleam" and No. 98, *To a Pedant*—are omitted from this discussion, although the texts have been printed along with that of No. 97 in an Appendix, and apparatus has been prepared from microfilm copies of Nos. 97 and 98. Fifty-one of the typewritten poems have only typewritten changes or no changes. In the remaining thirty-nine typed poems appear three handwritings: Dewey's, Alice Dewey's, and that of Adrienne Dewey Gay, Dewey's adopted daughter. Dewey's recognizable hand appears with the others on all but one of the thirty-nine, No. 95, which is annotated only by Adrienne Gay. Alice Dewey's comments and suggestions are in No. 47, *Creation;* Adrienne Gay's handwriting appears in eleven poems, clarifying faint letters and words, and penciling in suggestions such as "new parag." [1] In poem No. 92, a number of handwritten changes are in Dewey's characteristic hand; several others made with a different pen and in an awkward position have also been verified as his. The latter are compositional rather than simple clarifications or corrections and are similar to the kinds of alterations he made throughout the poetry.

No instances exist of a manuscript draft and a typed version of the same poem. Four poems, however, have at least two versions with degrees of variation; these variants are described in the sections of apparatus for the poems. Poems with more than one version are: Nos. 4, 24, 47, and 93. No. 4, "Generations of stifled worlds reaching out," has two typescripts on the same machine, both with Dewey's holograph corrections, one apparently a first draft. A second version of *When Thou Art Gone* is *Absence,* which is typed on a different machine and has minor variants. Variant parts of *Creation,* No. 47, appear in poems 31, 56, 57, and 77. No. 57, "Like fogs from some black cave of mournful night," is a rewritten version of the first section of *Creation;* No. 56, "Life blithe in lusty action restless and rude," is the beginning of another version of the second section of *Creation.* The first stanzas of No. 31 and No. 77 are almost identical: the first line of No. 31, "Long time lay the world level and open," appears as "Long time the world lay level and open" in the first stanza of No. 77. This repeated first stanza of both poems is related to Section I of *Creation* and the second stanza of No. 77 is a variant version of Section II of *Creation.* Two other poems embody similar treatment of a single theme; they are "Next spring earth will be all in green," (No. 93), and a less sophisticated version with the same theme, No. 95, "I should think th'earth would be ashamed." In addition, two retyped duplicates that cannot properly be labeled variant versions were typed on a machine that appears nowhere else in the collection nor in the John Dewey Papers; they are, "I wake from the long, long night," and "And shall we shut the door." The first is retyped perfectly; the second has two minor corrections in ink.

Six different typewriter faces appear in the poems. These are designated here and in the apparatus sections for the poems by arabic numbers; 1 and 2 are elite faces, 3–6 are pica. The number of poems in each face is: face 1—37; face 2—5; face 3—33; face 4—12; face 5—3; face 6—2 retyped duplicates.

---

1. The poems with Adrienne Dewey Gay's handwriting are: No. 2, *The Blossoming Wilderness;* No. 18, *Thy Mind;* No. 27, *The Child's Garden;* No. 31, "Long time lay the world level and open"; No. 32, *Mine Own Body;* No. 42, "Tho all the rhymes were long since rhymed"; No. 58, *A Moment and a Time;* No. 71, *Duplicity;* No. 91, "At night shining stars march in file"; No. 92, "John Banding looked and said"; No. 95, "I should think th'earth would be ashamed".

Four instances of the overlapping of two typewriter faces occur, and all are mixtures of faces 1 and 3. In one of these cases, a third face also appears: on No. 42, "Tho all the rhymes were long since rhymed," face 1 was used to make alterations and corrections in the poem, which is itself typed in face 3. At the foot of the page, upside down, appears the following, "35, the *way* of activity called for," in face 4, indicating that No. 42 was probably typed on a piece of paper left over from another task. The other instances of overlapping of type are these: No. 55, *A Journey*, face 1, is typewritten on the same page as No. 51, *A Fallow Field*, face 3; the first stanza of No. 31, mentioned above, "Long time lay the world level and open," is typed in face 3; when it is repeated as the first stanza of No. 77, face 1 is used. No. 19, *Ties*, is in face 3, and the title has been supplied in face 1.

Among the papers on which the poems are typed, four are linked in various ways with the typefaces thereon: all five poems in face 2 are on a wove paper watermarked *Hurd's Bank Note Bond*, the only instances of the use of this paper in the collection; the only typewriter face that appears on Columbia University letterhead stationery is face 1; with one exception, the poems typed in face 4 are on a wove paper watermarked *Efficiency Bond*, as is, in addition, one poem in face 5; face 3 is the only one that appears on a laid paper marked *Treasury Linen*, and all instances of the overlapping of faces 1 and 3 are on this paper except in Nos. 31 and 77, where the same first stanza appears in faces 3 and 1.

Fifteen of the ninety typewritten poems have no alterations.[2] Thirty-seven poems show varying amounts of only typewritten alteration; thirty-nine have either all holograph or a combination of holograph and typewritten alterations. Outside of the fifteen with no alterations, all the poems exhibit signs of composition, revision, retyping. The fifteen cleanly typed poems are undoubtedly final versions for which earlier drafts no longer exist; this hypothesis is based on two kinds of evidence: first, there is no indication that Dewey was given to copying out favorite poems by others,[3] and second, a high

2. The poems with no corrections or changes are: No. 7, *In Light*; No. 11, *One Night*; No. 15, *Swinburnian*; No. 17, *Thoughts*; No. 20, *Time Laid Low*; No. 21, *Two Joys*; No. 24, *When Thou Art Gone*; No. 26, *At the Last*; No. 35, *My Road*; No. 44, *To Death*; No. 55, *A Journey*; No. 63, *America*; No. 65, "And shall we shut the door"; No. 89, *Unfaith*; No. 95, "I should think th'earth would be ashamed".

3. In an early stage of the poetry study, the poetic works in Dewey's personal library were scrutinized for clues that he might have followed this practice, and a search of *Granger's Index* confirmed that none of the poems in the John Dewey Foundation collection had been anthologized. Numerous concordances, first-line indexes, and similar sources failed to provide any indication that the poems had been copied or published.

percentage of the other poems that do show signs of composition and change seem themselves to have been recopied from still earlier drafts. In a number of these, for instance, a line is continued with several words intended to start the next line; these are x'd-out at the end of the line and retyped without change at the intended place at the beginning of the following line, clearly suggesting the poem was being retyped from another document. Only eighteen poems seem not to have been retyped even once; not only are the evidences of composition in process more numerous in these poems but also they are characterized by the presence of trial lines in various places on the paper, by notations of possible rhyme schemes, and variant versions of single lines or couplets.

A uniform pattern of typewriting is apparent throughout the poems regardless of face; characteristic features of that pattern are: light pressure has been exerted on the shift key, causing special difficulty with capital letters (which often fail to print), with the apostrophe and '8', and with the double quotation mark and '2' (both on the same keys in manual typewriters at the time); substitution of 'd' for 's' and the reverse (a typical error made by an untrained typist), usually corrected at the typewriter; use of a single hyphen, or several, for the one-em dash, rather than the conventional two hyphens or single hyphen with space on either side; use of a single or double hyphen following other marks of punctuation, notably semicolons; interlineation of words, sometimes as corrections but more often as alterations; frequent interlineation of single letters inadvertently omitted; frequent spacing problems—running words together and leaving space between the letters of a word; the invariable use of a lower-case 'x' to delete material at the typewriter; a lack of decipherable regularity in the spacing for stanza breaks; and carelessness with left-hand margins, which causes a general slant to the right rather than any identifiable pattern of indentation.

The pointing is similarly consistent in all the poems regardless of face and more careful than the typewriting itself. Face 1 had an 'è' key that was regularly used; in the other typewriter faces, the accent was supplied by pen or pencil. Except for the apostrophe in contractions, which is generally omitted (Ive, een, neer, tis, twill)—probably because of difficulty with the shift key already mentioned—the pointing is scrupulous: periods mark the ends of complete sentences; semicolons are used for compound sentences; if punctuation is not present or is incorrect in the typed version, it is supplied by hand.

Spelling patterns are also regular and are characterized by the recurrence of the same errors or difficulties, usually corrected. A silent 'e' is frequently elided as in 'utterd' and 'hoverd'; words with intentionally elided vowels are often typed without apostrophe, as in 'uttrance', 'memry', 'blackning', 'langrous'.

Erroneous transpositions of 'e' and 'i' occur in nine instances, not always corrected: No. 2, 'counterfiet'; No. 58, 'thier'; No. 83, 'thier' corrected in pencil; No. 68 and No. 72, 'alien' *over* 'alein'; No. 82, 'firecely'; and in the trial lines written above No. 56, 'firce', 'wieir' *over* 'wier', and one apparently corrected 'weir'.

Especially noticeable is the difficulty caused by the word 'rhythm': No. 4, TMs[2], 'rhthym' (*first* 'h' *over* 'y'); No. 4, TMs[1], 'rythym'; No. 52 and No. 58, 'rythmic'; No. 73, 'rythmic' ('y' *in pencil over* 'h'); No. 77, 'rythmic', two instances.

Two additional unusual spelling forms appear: No. 23, 'prisioned' and No. 77, 'imprisioned'; No. 47, 'maddenned', and deleted from No. 83, 'saddenned'.

The numerous evidences of Dewey's composition revealed by the alterations and corrections he made in the poems provide, of course, the basic support for a conclusion that he wrote all the poems in the collection. In addition, even a cursory examination of non-poetry typescript material among his papers yields examples too numerous to cite of the same typewriting patterns, the pointing, and the "spelling" difficulties (which may simply be typewriting problems) that occur in the poetry.

For illustration, some examples of these similarities have been drawn from a single body of material: the extensive personally typed notes and letters that Dewey sent to Elsie Ripley Clapp, his assistant in two courses at Columbia University in 1911 and 1912.[4] Even though most of that material is simply running notes and summaries of class discussions—not reworked or retyped as were many of the poems—the time of writing coincides roughly with the presumed early period of Dewey's experimentation with writing poetry and the notes can serve as representative samples of typewriting practices. For instance, the difficulty with the shift key is apparent in the lightly printed, elevated, or absent capitals, the '8' for an intended apostrophe (and the omission of apostrophes in contractions), and the '2' for double quotation marks. All the other characteristic typing practices are also present: interlineations, often of words but even more often of single letters; the variable spacing within and between words; the use of 's' for 'd' and the reverse; the unvarying use of 'x' to delete; the correction of typewritten copy with both pen and pencil; the use of ink guidelines to place inserted material; and, perhaps most telling, 'happenned' (1 October 1911, letter); 'maddenned' (10 October 1911, Lecture 3); 'rythm' (21 October 1911, p. 3).

---

4. Elsie Ripley Clapp Papers, Special Collections, Morris Library, Southern Illinois University at Carbondale. Unless a specific collection is noted, materials cited in this discussion are in the John Dewey Papers, Special Collections, Morris Library.

## 2. Typewriters

Comparison of the typewriter faces used in the poetry with all Dewey's personally typed materials establishes the fact that the poems were typed on machines he owned or to which he had access, and, in all cases except face 6, machines on which he typed other notes and correspondence. Details about each typewriter appear in separate sections following this general discussion.

The earliest typescript by Dewey on a machine also used to type poetry is a set of his class lecture notes dated 1910; 1910 has therefore been assigned as the earliest known date for the typewritten poems. Dewey typed letters and other materials for a number of years before moving to Columbia University in 1904, but the machine used earlier in Chicago does not appear in any of the poetry. Although one or more of the typewriters used in the poetry may have been owned and used by Dewey before 1910, no physical evidence exists to verify that hypothesis.

The last year that any one of the typewriter faces found in the poetry appears among Dewey's other typewritten materials is 1928.[5] Dewey usually worked on two, and sometimes three, typewriters during a given period; only in 1910, and between 1924 and 1928, does a single typewriter also used for poetry appear in his other typewritten materials. Thus, although it is possible to set limiting dates for poetry typed on each machine, it is not possible to arrange the entire collection in exact chronological order. But, as the evidence also shows, beyond doubt more than two-thirds of the poems were typed between 1910 and 1918, even though a number of them may have been composed earlier and retyped during this period.[6]

5. The dates the poetry typewriters appear in other materials, along with the number of poems in each face, are the following:

| Face | Dates | Number of poems in face |
|------|-------|------------------------|
| 1 | 1910–1918 | 37 |
| 2 | 1911 | 5 |
| 3 | 1911–1916 | 33 |
| 4 | 1915–1928 | 12 |
| 5 | 1918–1923 | 3 |
| 6 | ? | 2 retyped duplicates |

6. The gradual progression, with overlapping, from one typewriter face to a succeeding one, is apparent in this table.

| Year | Face(s) |
|------|---------|
| 1910 | 1 |
| 1911 | 1,2,3 |
| 1912 | 1,3 |

Identification of the typewriters used in the poetry, and the exact dates they were used, is complicated somewhat by the practices of the Dewey family members—Alice, Lucy, Evelyn, and Jane—in the use of their typewriters. Each person typed correspondence and other materials, and, although different persons nominally owned certain machines, all borrowed freely. The machine with face 5 probably belonged to Evelyn; Dewey closed one 1918 letter on this typewriter with the statement that Evelyn wanted to go to bed and the machine was in her room.[7] Lucy identified the machine with face 4 as "Dad's machine" in a letter she typed on it at their Huntington, L. I., farm in September 1918.[8] The family practice of moving typewriters from place to place is illustrated by Dewey's having written a month earlier to Alice on this typewriter (face 4) from Philadelphia, saying that his machine had just arrived by express.[9] Between 1910, the year after the Deweys bought the farm at Huntington, and 1918, typewriter faces 1, 3, 4, and 5 appear in non-poetry materials typed by Dewey at the farm and at the Deweys' New York apartment, as well as at the Philadelphia location.

In addition to typewriter face 4, identified in 1918 by both Dewey and Lucy as that of his own machine, face 1 was on a machine he almost surely owned: between 1910 and 1918, he typed voluminous sets of class lecture notes, as well as correspondence and manuscript material, on this typewriter.

### *Typewriter face 1, elite, 1910–1918, 37 poems*

The earliest-dated non-poetry material typed by Dewey on a machine also used for poetry is the set of class notes with the typewritten date 19 October 1910. Most of the class notes and other material typed by Dewey between 1910 and 1915 are in this face.

| | |
|---|---|
| 1913 | 1,3 |
| 1914 | 1,3 |
| 1915 | 1,3,4 |
| 1916 | 1,3,4 |
| 1917 | 1,4 |
| 1918 | 1,4,5 [1919–1921, Dewey was in Japan and China; none of the typewriters appears.] |
| 1922 | 4,5 |
| 1923 | 4,5 |
| 1924–1928 | 4 |

7. John Dewey to Alice Dewey, 3 August 1918, John Dewey Papers.

8. Lucy Dewey to Alice and Jane Dewey, 9 September 1918, John Dewey Papers.

9. John Dewey to Alice Dewey, 9 August 1918, John Dewey Papers.

All poems in face 1 are either on Columbia University letterhead wove paper watermarked *W.S. & B. Paragon Linen / Made in U.S.A.* or on wove unmarked typing paper. Twelve of the thirty-seven have Dewey's handwritten corrections and changes. Complete carbon copies exist for two long poems in this face: No. 82, *A Peripatetic's Prayer* and No. 47, *Creation.* It is the ribbon copy of *Creation* that has extensive pencil comments in Alice Chipman Dewey's hand.[10]

*Typewriter face 2, elite, 1911, 5 poems*

The only examples of Dewey's typewriting of materials other than poetry on this machine are undated: one page of notes on ontological logic without date and mounted on plastic that prevents examination of the paper is among the John Dewey Papers, and two pages typed by Dewey, with holograph corrections, are in the Elsie Ripley Clapp Papers, also without date but among materials dated 1911. The period during which Dewey worked closely with Clapp, writing long letters and summaries of class discussions, was 1911–1912.

The five poems in this group are on white wove paper marked *Hurd's Bank Note Bond.* All have typewritten titles; only two have alterations, and the five could have been retyped at a single sitting.[11]

One poem in this face, No. 24, *When Thou Art Gone,* was among the poems re-discovered by Milton Halsey Thomas in 1973; like the other four in the group, it seems to have been retyped on a machine seldom used by Dewey. The probable earlier version of *When Thou Art Gone* is *Absence,* in typewriter face 1, which does not appear here as a sepa-

---

10. Poems in face 1 are: *Absence* (No. 24, *When Thou Art Gone*); No. 1, *Autumn;* No. 67, "Because the plan of world is dim and blurred"; No. 68, *Borrowed;* No. 70, *But;* No. 47, *Creation;* No. 71, *Duplicity;* No. 49, "Earth-born dust rising in the air"; No. 52, "From my glance backward sent recedes"; No. 95, "I should think th'earth would be ashamed"; No. 7, *In Light;* No. 54, *Indian Summer at the Farm;* No. 55, *A Journey;* No. 75, "Language, fourth dimension of the mind"; No. 56, "Life blithe in lusty action restless and rude"; No. 57, "Like fogs from some black cave of mournful night"; No. 31, "Long time lay the world level and open"; No. 32, *Mine Own Body;* No. 58, *A Moment and a Time;* No. 59, *The Mountain's Hour;* No. 35, *My Road;* No. 10, *Natural Magic;* No. 93, "Next spring earth will be all in green"; No. 36, "Not now thy scourging rod"; No. 82, *A Peripatetic's Prayer;* No. 13, *The Round of Passion;* No. 14, *Song;* No. 15, *Swinburnian;* No. 41, "That frail ship I load with limitless freight"; No. 94, *This Child's Garden of Verse;* No. 17, *Thoughts;* No. 18, *Thy Mind;* No. 20, *Time Laid Low;* No. 87, *Truth's Torch;* No. 46, *Two Births;* No. 88, "Two extremes of one joinèd theme"; No. 21, *Two Joys;* No. 89, *Unfaith.*

11. Poems in face 2 are: No. 26, *At the Last;* No. 11, *One Night;* No. 39, *Respite;* No. 23, *The Unending Hours;* No. 24, *When Thou Art Gone.*

rately numbered poem but is discussed in a note to *When Thou Art Gone.*

### Typewriter face 3, pica, 1911–1916, 33 poems

Three long non-poetry examples of Dewey's typing on this machine are among the John Dewey Papers and in three other correspondence collections. In the Dewey Papers is a set of undated notes on Bergson, laid in a 1911 edition of *Matter and Memory.* The notes refer to *Matter and Memory* and were working material for his review of H. S. R. Elliott's *Modern Science and the Illusions of Professor Bergson;* that review was published in *Philosophical Review* 21 (1912): 705–7. Also in the Dewey Papers is an eleven-page typescript of notes on "Chapman's Pol. Econ.," a work published in 1912; following those notes on Chapman are six and one-half pages with the heading "Final," also on political economics.

In the Horace Kallen Papers, American Jewish Archives, Cincinnati, Ohio, are two letters in this typeface by Dewey, one from the Huntington farm dated 22 September 1913, and another with Columbia University typed at the head, dated 13 December 1913. He typed a letter from Huntington on this machine to Scudder Klyce on 4 April 1916 (Scudder Klyce Papers, Manuscripts Division, Library of Congress), and one to A. B. Hart on 9 June 1914 (Dewey Letters Collection, Rutgers University, New Brunswick, N.J.).

Although no other examples of Dewey's typing on the machine with typewriter face 3 have been located, the large proportion of poems in this face (33)—as well as the intermediate stage of composition shown in most of them—suggests that it was a machine to which he had access during periods of relative leisure, with time enough to experiment and when regular professional tasks were minimal.

The same mixture of type between faces 3 and 1 that is found in four examples of the poetry also occurs in the second set of reading notes on Chapman, "Final," mentioned above. One page of these face 3 notes (p. 2) has corrections and interpolations typed in face 1 on the front and almost a full page in face 1 on the back. Page 2a is completely in face 1, and the remaining three pages go back to face 3.

This particular combination of faces in both poetry and in a non-poetry typescript strongly supports the other evidences of Dewey's authorship of the poems: the possibility of another person's having followed the same pattern seems unlikely. In all cases of the appearance of faces 1 and 3 on the same document—poetry and non-poetry—the basic face is 3; face 1 is used for corrections, changes, and additions. This pattern suggests that the face 1 typing may have been done when the typewriter with face 3 was no longer available.

All instances of the mixture of typewriter faces are on a laid paper marked *Treasury Linen,* and no other faces appear on this paper. In addition to those with both faces 1 and 3 (Nos. 19, 31, 42, 51), the four others on *Treasury Linen* with only face 3 are Nos. 9, 43, 61, and 84. The remaining poems in face 3 are on lined paper, probably examination books, and on typewriter paper like that also used in face 1 poems. A number of poems in face 3 were typed when the machine apparently had a very worn ribbon; the typescripts are so faint as to be hardly legible.[12]

*Typewriter face 4, pica, 1915–1928, 12 poems*

This face appears most frequently from 1915 up to 1928 in material other than poetry typed by Dewey. It is the only face of the six poetry faces found in other materials typed after Dewey's return from China in 1921.

Among the John Dewey Papers are three long typescripts in face 4 on *Efficiency Bond,* as are all but one of the poems typewritten in this face. A set of personally typed 1917 class notes for "Psychological Ethics" and a fifteen-page draft for Dewey's article, "The Objects of Valuation," which was published in the *Journal of Philosophy* 15 (1918): 253–58, are both on paper sidemarked *Efficiency Bond.* Another set of notes with the heading "For T. C. Course, 1917" has the *Efficiency Bond* center mark.

Two kinds of wove paper have the *Efficiency Bond / A.P. & P. Co.* mark; in each the mark is the same size, but the papers are of different weights and the mark is placed differently. In the lighter-weight paper, the mark appears twice on the edge of the sheet, often with only the second line visible. In the heavier paper, the mark is centered. Poem No. 62, "The rope is cut, the anchor falls," has the

12. Poems in face 3 are: No. 25, "Across the white of my mind's map"; No. 63, *America;* No. 64, "And high God on his throne"; No. 65, "And the lad eager replied: No sir, not a God damned Word"; No. 91, "At night shining stars march in file"; No. 2, *The Blossoming Wilderness;* No. 69, *Brave Things;* No. 27, *The Child's Garden;* No. 72, *Education;* No. 51, *A Fallow Field;* No. 73, *Forgetfulness;* No. 5, *Hope and Memory;* No. 8, "Is this the end?"; No. 92, "John Banding looked and said"; No. 76, *Life;* No. 30, *Little Things;* No. 77, "Long time the world lay level and open"; No. 78, *The March;* No. 79, "Meadows of the dawn are curtained in dusk"; No. 9, *My Body and My Soul;* No. 33, *My Fever;* No. 37, "Not wrinkled, shrivelled, grey"; No. 60, "Now night, mother soul, broods the weary hours"; No. 81, *Paradise Lost and Regained;* No. 61, *Renewal;* No. 83, "Rough mountains once were freedom's home"; No. 84, *Sorolla;* No. 42, "Tho all the rhymes were long since rhymed"; No. 85, "Tho some of the pretty blushing ladies were shocked"; No. 86, "Through windy gorges of the clouds"; No. 19, *Ties;* No. 43, *To Conscience;* No. 45, "To us you came from out of dark".

side mark on both its pages; all others are on the centermarked *Efficiency Bond*. Apparently both kinds of *Efficiency Bond* paper were in use about the same time in 1917 and 1918; the poems in typewriter face 4 were probably either composed or retyped also at this time. Both poems quoted by Anzia Yezierska in her published novels are in this face and on *Efficiency Bond*.

In addition to the twelve numbered poems in face 4, there is one duplicate, which is Dewey's second draft of poem No. 4, "Generations of stifled worlds reaching out." This second draft, incorporating Dewey's handwritten alterations from the first draft, was one of the five poems Halsey Thomas sent to the Dewey Center in 1973. It is on heavy yellow unmarked wove paper; the original first draft is on wove paper watermarked *Efficiency Bond*. The one face 4 poem not on *Efficiency Bond* (No. 29, "Last night I stood upon the hill"), found among the Dewey Papers correspondence, is on wove paper with a faint watermark picturing two castles.

This machine, the typewriter Dewey identified as his own and used more than any other from 1915 through 1928, accounts for a relatively small number of poems—only 12, as compared to the 37 in face 1 and the 33 in face 3. This fact lends weight to the hypothesis that his interest in writing poetry peaked before he went to Japan and China in 1919 and that little, if any, poetry was written after his return.[13]

*Typewriter face 5, pica, 1918, 1923, 3 poems*

This face appears infrequently among materials typed by Dewey; as mentioned, the machine apparently belonged to Evelyn Dewey and was used by Dewey at the Huntington farm from time to time, although one letter to S. O. Levinson with the carbon of a three-page statement dated 11 February 1923 is headed with Dewey's apartment address (S. O. Levinson Papers, Manuscript Division, Library of Congress). A single page of notes for the Carus Lectures (1922) is the only other non-poetry example of this face located.

Two poems in this face are on heavy wove unmarked paper; they are No. 38, *Pulse in an Earthen Jar,* and No. 44, *To Death.* The third, No. 22, *Two Weeks,* written to Anzia Yezierska, is on *Efficiency Bond.*

13. Poems in face 4 are: No. 65, "And shall we shut the door"; No. 48, "Dear moon and stars, and dearer yet"; No. 50, "Fair flowers grow in my garden ground"; No. 4, "Generations of stifled worlds reaching out"; No. 28, "He failed. Though he was strong"; No. 6, "I wake from the long, long night"; No. 53, *In the Country;* No. 29, "Last night I stood upon the hill"; No. 80, *The New World;* No. 40, *Romance;* No. 62, "The rope is cut, the anchor falls"; No. 16, "There stirred within me".

*Typewriter face 6, pica, date unknown, 2 duplicates*

Among the poems in the collection were clean copies of No. 65, "And shall we shut the door," and No. 6, "I wake from the long, long night," both on a laid unmarked paper with chains 25 mm. apart as in the paper marked *Treasury Linen.* The originals of both poems are on *Efficiency Bond* and were among the five found by Halsey Thomas in 1973.

Dewey's characteristic typewriting pattern is not apparent in these two poems, and the retyped version of "I wake" does not incorporate his handwritten changes from the original. Thomas thinks he may well have made the retyped versions himself at some now-forgotten date.[14]

14. Thomas to Boydston, 26 July 1974.

# Editorial Method

The ninety-five poems in the John Dewey Foundation collection, and the three Appendix poems copied by Gérard Deledalle, have been printed in clear text for the convenience of the general reader. Dewey's typewriting was unskilled and erratic even on poems apparently retyped from drafts; since ninety-two of the poems are typewritten, a number of changes have been made in accidentals (punctuation, spelling, capitalization) and in formal matters (capitalization of titles, spacing, typeovers) to prepare the clear text. These changes are basically of two kinds: correction and regularization. To avoid undue emphasis in the emendations list on regularizations, two kinds of editorial changes have been grouped in class lists preceding the apparatus for the individual poems. These are the removal of final periods from titles and the regularization of Dewey's use of apostrophes.

The following changes and corrections in formal matters have been made without notice: printing titles in upper and lower case letters; correcting faulty spacing between and within words; substituting one-em dashes where Dewey often had a single hyphen, and sometimes three or four; supplying partially missing letters; regularizing the contraction 'th' ' to be closed up before vowels and spaced preceding consonants; and accepting Dewey's own corrections of typographical errors, whether by typing over or marking over by hand. Such corrections are, however, recorded as alterations when any possibility exists that the "error" might have been another word or the start of another word rather than a simple typographical mistake.

Most of the poems have irregularly slanting indentions predominantly from upper left to lower right. When no decipherable pattern exists, the clear text is printed with all lines flush-left. When a pattern is apparent, even though not completely consistent, it has been followed faithfully here. Similarly, unless Dewey's intention to establish stanzas is clear, no stanza breaks appear. When stanzaic patterns can be discerned, they have regularly been followed in the clear text.

The editorial apparatus for each poem is arranged by ascending numbers as the poems appear in this volume. For each poem the apparatus includes: a physical description of typescript or manuscript; variants (where more than one text exists); emendations; alterations; and, where appropriate, explanatory notes.

In the apparatus for each poem, titles assigned by Dewey are set in italics whether they were underlined, typewritten in full capitals, or typed in upper and lower-case letters. In the absence of a title, the clear text first line of the poem appears in double quotation marks after the poem number, but without any final punctuation.

After the title appears the physical description of the typescript or manuscript: typewriter face; kind and size of paper; variant texts; identification of copy-text where variants exist; and symbols used for variant texts.

In the emendations section for each poem appears every change from the copy-text typescript or manuscript in both substantives and accidentals, except the kinds of corrections and regularizations described above. In the emendations list, page-line references are to the clear text as printed in the present edition; the reading to the left of the bracket, the lemma, is that of the printed text. For emendations limited to punctuation, the curved dash ~ means the same word(s) as before the bracket; the inferior caret ∧ signals the lack of a punctuation mark. If the source of the emendation is not identified by a symbol, the emendation has been made editorially for this edition.

Following the list of emendations, Dewey's alterations to the typescripts and manuscripts are recorded;[1] unless noted, all alterations to manuscripts are handwritten and alterations to typescripts are typewritten. The reading to the left of the bracket is that of the printed text; in all cases where this clear text reading represents an emended copy-text reading, it is preceded by a single grid # to direct the reader's attention to the copy-text reading in the emendations list. If the lemma includes a word in which the placement of the apostrophe has been regularized, a double grid ## signals the fact that the word appears in the Regularization of Apostrophes list. In all readings quoted to the right of the square bracket in the alterations list, and in all trial lines transcribed in apparatus notes, the original typescript or manuscript reading is reproduced exactly in all respects, except that, as noted, Dewey's own corrections of his typographical errors do not appear.

In the notation of alterations, a semicolon means that the notation after the semicolon, even when separated from the lemma by an intervening notation, refers back to the lemma itself. For example, No. 43.11, endless] *in ink above del.* 'unceasing'; *after ink-interl. then del.* 'this' shows that the interlined word 'endless' rather than 'unceasing' appears after the deleted interlined 'this'. The abbreviation *del.* is used to show material marked out in ink except when pencil is specif-

---

1. This method of transcribing variants and alterations is derived and adapted from a system developed by Fredson Bowers, which he describes in "Transcription of Manuscripts: The Record of Variants," *Studies in Bibliography* 29 (1976): 212–64.

ically mentioned; any alteration noted as *added* is also in ink unless pencil is specified. For material deleted at the typewriter, *x'd-out* is used. On one poem, No. 29, "Last night I stood upon the hill," all alterations except x'd-out words were made by hand and in pencil; notice to this effect is given in the headnote, and in this case only, the medium is not specified for each entry. The abbreviation *alt.* is used to identify material altered in some way from an earlier form; if altered by hand, the medium is given; if medium is not mentioned, it is to be assumed the alteration was typewritten. For example, No. 72.11, Until] *alt. in pencil from* 'Till' is the form of notation used to show that 'Un' was penciled in before 'Till'; the 'T' was made lowercase, and the final 'l' deleted in pencil. *Over* means inscribed over original letters, not interlined; *above* means interlined without a caret unless a caret is specified. When an addition is a simple interlineation, the formula is *interl.* or *interl. w. caret.* When a deletion positions the interlineation, *interl.* is dropped and the formula reads *above del.* 'xyz' or *w. caret above del.* 'xyz'. All carets were made by hand; when a caret accompanies a typewritten interlineation, it is in ink unless pencil is noted. When carets are used with handwritten alterations, they are in the same medium as the alteration.

In brief, with respect to medium, only the abbreviation *del.* and the words *added* and *caret* always apply to handwritten changes made in ink unless pencil is specified; in all other instances—*above, over, inserted, interl., alt., below, before, after*—the change was made at the typewriter unless the medium is specified. For example, in No. 57.2 uncertain] *after del.* 'from', both 'from' and 'uncertain' are typewritten, but 'from' has been marked out in ink. If, on the other hand, 'uncertain' had been added in ink, the alteration would have read: uncertain] *added after del.* 'from', and the medium would be assumed as ink in both *added* and *del.* notations. Inasmuch as most such additions are interlined, the medium will ordinarily appear, as in *interl. in ink* or *interl. in pencil.* Use of *interl.* alone always means a typewritten interlineation. The words *before* and *after* signal a change made on the same line, whether original line or interline, as in No. 25.14, sculptured] *after x'd-out* 'stand' where both 'sculptured' and 'stand' are on the main line, in contrast with No. 43.11, endless] *in ink above del.* 'unceasing'; *after ink-interl. then del.* 'this' where both 'endless' and 'this' are still on the same line, but this time, in an interlineation above 'unceasing', which is on the original main line.

When an alteration, usually of a word or two, has been typed or written directly below the original line, the formula is *below* 'xyz'. The word *inserted* refers to marginal additions that cannot be called interlines but are of the same nature. In alterations involving more than one line, and in transcriptions of trial lines, the solidus / signals the end of a line.

Several instances occur of these revised lines or trial lines that

95

Dewey deleted from the final version of a poem; these are transcribed with all revisions shown in brackets. To clarify what words in the text are affected by the description in the square brackets, an asterisk is placed before the first word to which the bracketed description applies. For example, in a trial line for poem No. 66, the transcription reads: And through the tears *with which [*above x'd-out* 'that'] th['e' *x'd-out*] old mans eyes. In the example, the two words 'with which' have been typed in above the one x'd-out word 'that'.

The asterisk is not used in unambiguous circumstances when only a single word is affected and this word comes immediately after a bracketed entry (as in 'th' above), or when an alteration occurs at the beginning of a transcription, as in the following: ['Oer' *x'd-out*] Flooding ['F' *over* 'f'] the sky's pent wieir.

In cases where a line has been revised and then revised again, the asterisk is used as illustrated above, and small brackets distinguish subsidiary revisions from the main alterations covered by the asterisk, as in the trial line for No. 56, 'Poured firce black torrents straight and sheer', which was altered at least twice in revision and is transcribed thus: Poured firce *⌈'the' *x'd-out*⌉ black [*above x'd-out* 'floods of'] ['floods' *x'd-out*] torrents straight and sheer. As the transcription shows, the x'd-out 'the' in small brackets is part of the interlineation above the x'd-out 'floods of'; the asterisk therefore applies to it and also to 'black'. The process of revision was probably this: the first version began 'Poured firce floods of'; 'floods of' was x'd-out and 'floods' typed in, then x'd-out, and 'torrents' was substituted. Before finishing the line, Dewey interlined 'the black', probably applying to 'floods' but possibly to 'torrents' and, finally, 'the' was x'd-out.

The final version of such transcribed lines can be read easily by following from start to finish all words outside the brackets. Regular size brackets show pure deletions, positioned by the asterisk. Corrections and alterations in the deleted material within these regular brackets, as well as subsidiary revisions in small brackets, can be studied separately as can their relation to the final version.

The last section in the apparatus for each poem is, where appropriate, a note in which are described and discussed variant versions of the poems, historical evidence, internal references, and similar information.

# Regularization Lists

## 1: Titles

A final period has been deleted from the titles of poems with the following numbers: 2, 5, 7, 9, 11, 12, 13, 18, 19, 20, 27, 32, 33, 35, 38, 46, 47, 54, 58, 59, 61, 63, 72, 73, 76, 81, 84, 89, 94.

## 2: Apostrophes

Dewey frequently elided an 'e' that would have been silent anyway, substituting an apostrophe, as in 'surrender'd'. He also often used the apostrophe to eliminate a regularly sounded letter, as in 'mem'ry' and 'wond'ring'. However, he apparently failed at times to exert sufficient pressure on the shift key to type the apostrophe rather than the figure '8'. This difficulty caused in some instances the figure '8' rather than the apostrophe to appear, and led to the omission of the apostrophe in other instances where his intention to use it was clear from the numerous parallel cases. The apostrophe has therefore been regularly restored in '-ed' and '-ing' forms where a letter is omitted as a sign of intended elision, and has been inserted where necessary in contractions—'eer', 'Ive', 'tis', 'twill'. All such regularizations appear in the list that follows; if the addition of an apostrophe makes a possessive form, it appears in the Emendations list, as at 66.4, man's] mans.

| | | | |
|---|---|---|---|
| 2.3 | ling'ring] lingring | 16.25 | whene'er] wheneer |
| 2.12 | 'Twas] Twas | 16.26 | ling'ring] lingring |
| 2.18 | lab'ring] labring | 17.2 | Silk'n] Silkn |
| 2.20 | 'Twas] Twas | 17.3 | Hover'd] Hoverd |
| 4.3 | utt'rance] uttrance | 18.6 | ling'ring] lingring |
| 5.8 | mem'ry's] memry's | 19.3 | 'Tis] Tis |
| 6.7 | I'm] Im | 19.17 | Scat'red] Scatred |
| 8.18 | op'ning] opning | 20.4 | I'll] Ill |
| 9.3,7 | 'tis] tis | 22.4,9 | I've] Ive |
| 9.7 | 'twill] twill | 22.30 | Whate'er] Whateer |
| 15.9 | smoth'ring] smothring | 22.30 | howe'er] howeer |
| 15.15 | surrender'd] surrenderd | 22.98 | hung'ring] hungring |
| 16.24 | trait'rous] traitrous | 24.4 | ling'ring] lingr'ing |

| | | | |
|---|---|---|---|
| 29.17 | Tho't] Thot | 67.17 | happ'd] happed |
| 29.24 | silver'd] silverd | 70.16 | O'er] Oer |
| 31.6 | swoll'n] swolln | 71.11 | hidd'n] hiddn |
| 32.6 | uplab'ring] uplabring | 72.14 | whisp'ring] whispring |
| 32.17 | o'erstrained] oerstrained | 72.21 | o'erdecked] oe'rdecked |
| 34.1 | gutt'ring] gut'tring | 72.30 | 'twas] twas |
| 36.4 | ling'ring] lingring | 72.57 | e'en] een |
| 36.6 | E'en] Een | 72.58 | ne'er] neer |
| 36.18 | E'en] Eeen | 73.6 | slurr'd] slurrd |
| 36.19 | 'Tis] Tis | 74.11 | O'er] Oer |
| 41.5 | ne'er] neer | 75.18 | whisper'd] whisperd |
| 41.10 | 'Twere] Twere | 75.22 | mutt'ring] muttring |
| 46.2 | fever'd] feverd | 77.18 | ne'er] neer |
| 46.18 | 'gainst] gainst | 78.11 | sund'ring] sundring |
| 46.26 | unshelter'd] unshelterd | 78.13 | slumb'ring] slumbring |
| 46.29 | e'en] een | 79.5 | threat'ning] threatning |
| 47.2 | show'ring] showring | 80.18 | untrav'lled] untravlled |
| 47.15 | untemper'd] untemperd | 81.3 | 'Twas] Twas |
| 47.22 | Lang'rous] Langrous | 81.12 | 'tis] tis |
| 47.24 | scatter'd] scatterd | 81.17 | e'en] een |
| 47.38 | o'ercharged] oercharged | 81.35 | that's] thats' |
| 47.47 | black'ning] blackning | 82.23,37 | e'en] een |
| 49.6 | gold'n] goldn | 82.33 | Wand'ring] Wandrin |
| 49.12 | 'Gainst] Gainst | 83.3 | men's] mens' |
| 49.12 | heav'n] heavn | 87.3 | scatter'd] scatterd |
| 50.8 | flow'r's] flowr's | 88.6 | dev'lish] devlish |
| 51.4 | till'd] tilld | 88.9 | off'ring] offring |
| 52.4 | o'er] oer | 89.13 | 'tis] tis |
| 52.17 | unspok'n] unspokn | 92.40 | I'm] Im |
| 52.18 | utter'd] utterd | 93.4 | ragg'd] raggd |
| 56.5 | Unsob'red] Unsobred | 94.7 | 'tis] tis |
| 60.2 | Flutt'ring] Fluttring | 94.10 | can't] cant |
| 60.5 | sund'ring] sundring | 97.3 | Wand'ring] Wandring |
| 61.5 | indiff'rent] indif'frent | 98.2 | 'Tis] Tis |
| 67.2 | utter'd] utterd | 98.21 | gather'd] gatherd |

## 3: Stanza Breaks

Stanza breaks coincide with the ends of the following pages: 18, 21, 27, 36, 47, 49, 50, 52, 65, 71, 72, 73, 77.

# Apparatus for Poems

## 1. *Autumn* (TMs)

Typewriter face 1; wove unmarked paper, Columbia University letterhead, 176 x 198 mm., trimmed

*Alterations:*
    4 blooms] *after del.* 'buds and'
    4 th'] 'e' *x'd-out; apostrophe added*
    8 fair] *interl. w. caret*

## 2. *The Blossoming Wilderness* (TMs)

Typewriter face 3; wove unmarked paper, 183 x 249 mm., trimmed

*Emendations:*
    2 joyous] jouyous
    2 counterfeit] counterfiet
    5 lo,] ~∧
    6 broad] brozd
    6 meadows] mendows
    7 obedient] obedi'ent
    10 kisses] kixses
    11 pleasure] plezsure
    13 lovelier] lovlier
    22 searched] searced
    22 unknown] unknwon

*Alterations:*
    2 in] *alt. from* 'on'
    3 flower paved] *above* 'flower' *partly over* 'garden' *and* 'paved'
    4 And] *inserted*
    4 perfume] 'P' *x'd-out,* 'p' *not added*
    4 space] *after x'd-out* 'its'
    5 Do] *above x'd-out* 'Did'
 #5 lo, a] *above x'd-out* 'lo, a'
    5 path] *before x'd-out* 'led'

5 leads] *interl. after undel.* 'a'
6 Opening] *alt. from* 'Opened'
8 and playful] *above x'd-out* 'beside'
9 peaceful] *above x'd-out* 'sweeping'
9 singing] *above x'd-out* 'pearly'
10 as] *interl.*
10 to] *over* 'in'
16 sun-lit] *after x'd-out* 'were'
16 and] *interl.*
18 but] *alt. from* 'by'
25 Thus] *inserted before x'd-out* 'For' *and illegible word*
25 sweet] *interl.*
25 idly] *interl.*
25 drawn] *after x'd-out* 'sweet'
25 fondling] *after x'd-out* 'kiss'
26 Awoke] *over* 'Awakes'
26 love's] *before x'd-out* 'constant service.'

## 3. "Empty as high heaven's heartless shell" (MS)

Wove paper marked *W. S. & B. Paragon Linen / Made in U.S.A.*, Columbia University letterhead, 182 x 268 mm., trimmed

*Emendations:*
6 warm,] ~∧
8 As] as

*Alterations:*
4 waves move] *above del.* 'move waves'
5 like] *over* 'as'
7 as windswept] *w. caret above del.* 'like'
7 light] *after del.* 'vibrant'
8 As] *after undel. illegible word*

## 4. "Generations of stifled worlds reaching out" (TMss)

TMs[1] Typewriter face 4; wove paper marked *Efficiency Bond,* 212 x 140 mm.
TMs[2] Typewriter face 4; heavy yellow unmarked paper, 178 x 131 mm., torn
AY    in *All I Could Never Be* by Anzia Yezierska (New York: Brewer, Warren & Putnam, 1932), p. 41.

Copy-text is TMs[2], a later revision of TMs[1], with the final handwritten line of TMs[1] typed and several erroneous spellings corrected.

*Variants:*
  1 worlds∧] words, AY
  2 Through you,] *included in line 1* TMs[1]; *through you*∧
   *included in line 1* AY
 ##3 utt'rance] utterance TMs[1], AY
  5 have,] ~∧ TMs[1]
  6 dumb, smothered] dumb, inchoate AY
  7 Inchoate, unutterable] Unutterable AY
  7 mine,] ~∧ AY
  9 slow∧revolving] ~ - ~ AY
  10 be them,] ~. AY
  11 the] thy AY
  12 great song] song AY
  13 I∧] ~, AY
  13 see,] ~∧ AY
  16 distance] distances TMs[1]
  18 horizons] horizon AY
  19 the generations] generations TMs[1]
  20 Of the dawn] *included in line 18* AY

*Emendations:*
  6 smothered] somothered
  9 rhythm] rhthym

*Alterations in* TMs[2]:
  1 worlds] *w. caret above x'd-out* 'generations'
  2+ [x'd-out line]] 'Aching on lips that have died,'
  3 lips∧] *comma del.*
  17 old] *w. guideline below* 'world'
  18+ [x'd-out false start]] 'Tremuble with'
  19 the] *interl. in ink w. caret*


## 5. *Hope and Memory* (TMs)

Typewriter face 3; lined examination book paper, 125 x 210 mm., trimmed

*Alteration:*
  8 still might] *above undel.* 'might still'


## 6. "I wake from the long, long night" (TMss)

TMs[1] Typewriter face 4; wove paper marked *Efficiency Bond,* 211
  x 280 mm.
TMs[2] Typewriter face 6; laid paper, chains 23 mm. apart, 167 x
  230 mm., trimmed

AY    *Red Ribbon on a White Horse* by Anzia Yezierska (New
        York: Charles Scribner's Sons, 1950), pp. 111–12.
Copy-text is TMs[1]
AY:

> I arise from a long, long night of thoughtless
>     dreams,
> Joyless, griefless begins the web of unillumined
>     duties,
> A silken web in which I'm bound.
>     Earthward my eyes,
> Lest your spirit keep me from the pact with my
>     possessions
> And lure me to your wilderness of tears,
> Where no harvest shall I reap, save stabs and
>     flames of pain
> And wan exhaustion, among the unshepherded
>     sheep of thought
> Who travel through trackless wilds of untamed
>     desire.

*Variants in TMss:*

   7 Im] I'm
   8 Earth ward] Earthward
   9 tramelled] trammeled
  13 stern∧eyed] ~ - ~
  19 Exhaustions] Exhaustion
  19 th'unshepherded] the unshepherded
  20 th'untracked] through untracked
  22 grave ∧] ~,
  22 treasure] treasures

*Emendations:*

   8 Earthward] TMs²; Earth ward
   9 trammeled] TMs²; tramelled
  13 stern-eyed] TMs²; ~∧~
  22 cooped-in] ~∧~

*Alterations:*

   2 fancies ∧] *comma pencil-del.*
   4 The] *after x'd-out* 'the'
   5 begins] 's' *added in pencil*
  11 And] *above* 'And' *over* 'Till'
  11 my] *above* 'my' *over* 'the'
  15+ [x'd-out false start]] 'Of hornrtrtress'
  17 From] ('F' *in pencil over* 'f'); *after pencil-del.* 'And'
  19 among] *after x'd-out* 'agined'

19 th'] 'e' *x'd-out before apostrophe*
20 th'] *interl.* 'e' *x'd-out before apostrophe*
20 wild] *final* 's' *x'd-out*
21 desire] *final* 's' *pencil-del.*
21+ [*x'd-out false start*]] 'To my ['a' *interl., x'd-out*] cooped in grave'
22 smothered] *after x'd-out* 'by my'
22 the] *in ink over* 'a'

## 7. *In Light* (TMs)

Typewriter face 1; wove unmarked paper, approximately 98 x 178 mm., untrimmed, torn at top and right side

*Alteration:*
3 sky] *before x'd-out* 'to lo'

## 8. "Is this the end?" (TMs)

Typewriter face 3; lined examination book paper, 145 x 175 mm., trimmed at bottom

*Emendations:*
5 fleeting] flee ing
20 rend,] ~.

*Alterations:*
2 with a closing door] *below x'd-out* 'from which there pours'
3 Thru which] *inserted before x'd-out* 'Whence'
3 I] *before del.* 'may'
4 of] *interl.*
5 A] *inserted before x'd-out* 'memry s'
19 Dear] *inserted before x'd-out* 'Great'
19 more ∧] *period x'd-out*

## 9. *My Body and My Soul* (TMs)

Typewriter face 3; laid paper marked *Treasury Linen,* chains 23 mm. apart, 187 × 206 mm.

*Emendation:*
4 Love] love

*Alterations:*
5 no] *final* 'w' *x'd-out*
6 willing, love goes] *w. caret above x'd-out and del. illegible word*

103

15 ghost,] *comma added*
15 self,] *comma added*
16 body's] *after x'd-out* 'the'
16 other's] ' 's' *added*
16 his] *alt. in ink from* 'its'

## 10. *Natural Magic* (TMs)

Typewriter face 1; wove unmarked paper, 192 x 189 mm.

*Emendations:*
10 crescent] creseent
12 Of] of

*Alterations:*
19 flowers'] *before x'd-out* 'perfum'
23 the] *over* 'as'

## 11. *One Night* (TMs)

Typewriter face 2; wove paper, probably marked *Hurd's Bank Note Bond* ['Hur' at left edge], 175 x 252 mm., trimmed

## 12. *Postponement* (MS)

Black ink; wove paper marked *W. S. & B. Paragon Linen* / *Made in U.S.A.*, Columbia University letterhead, 176 x 171 mm.; on same sheet as No. 34

*Emendation:*
6 swim.] ~—

*Alterations:*
3 And now] *over* 'I guess'
5 faint] *after del.* 'so'

## 13. *The Round of Passion* (TMs)

Typewriter face 1; wove unmarked paper, 168 x 214 mm., trimmed

*Alteration:*
0.1 Passion.] *in ink over* 'Fire'

## 14. *Song* (TMs)

Typewriter face 1; wove unmarked paper, 160 x 170 mm., trimmed

*Emendation:*
> 2 red-topped] redtopped

*Alterations:*
> 6+ [*x'd-out line*]] 'Bleak earth puts on its'
> 7 In brightness] *above x'd-out* 'Olive'
> 10 may] 'a' *over* 'i'

## 15. *Swinburnian* (TMs)

Typewriter face 1; wove unmarked paper, 166 x 190 mm., trimmed

## 16. "There stirred within me" (TMs)

Typewriter face 4; wove paper marked *Efficiency Bond,* two sheets: 187 x 280 mm., 194 x 239 mm.

*Emendations:*
> 7 assembled] asembled
> 9 spoke:] ~∧
> 31 opened.] ~,

*Alterations:*
> 4 murdered,] *comma added in pencil*
> 8 tread] *above x'd-out* 'approach'
> 18 quick] *interl.*
> 19 every] *after x'd-out* 'from'
> 19 sealèd] *accent added in pencil*
> 20 By] *after x'd-out* 'That'
> 21 spoke] *above x'd-out* 'told'
> 23 Desire] *interl. in pencil w. caret*
> 23 till] 't' *in pencil over* 'T'
> 31 its pages] *in pencil above pencil-del.* 'twas'
> 35 Where] *before x'd-out* 'no'
> 35 from dumb] *in pencil over* 'in stricken'
> 35 now] *interl.*
> 41 faith] *before pencil-del.* 'that that'
> 44 glory] *above x'd-out* 'greatness'

## 17. *Thoughts* (TMs)

Typewriter face 1; wove unmarked paper, 168 x 108 mm., trimmed; on same sheet as No. 21

## 18. *Thy Mind* (TMs)

Typewriter face 1; wove unmarked paper, 180 x 170 mm.

105

*Emendations:*
    5 mountain] mounatin
    9 dignity,] ~.
    10 mystery.] ~∧

*Alterations:*
    2 wind;] *before x'd-out* 'Beauteous mo'
    3 Transparent] *in ink above del.* 'beauteous'
    3 things,] *comma added*
    5 some] *interl.*
    6 sun] *interl. w. caret*
    6 rays] *before x'd-out* 'of sun'
    7 Thy] ('T' *in ink over* 't'); *after del.* 'Thus'
    7 faithful mind] *in ink w. caret above del.* 'thoughts'
    7 clear] *after del.* 'so'
    8+ [*del. line*]] 'Draws ['D' *and* 's' *in ink*] from those far ['ben-ig' *x'd-out*] depths a mystery'
    9 Draws] *in ink over* 'And'
    9 its] *in ink over* 'their'
    10 And . . . mystery] *added*

## 19. *Ties* (TMs)

Typewriter face 3 (title, typewriter face 1); laid paper marked *Treasury Linen,* chains 25 mm. apart, 215 x 158 mm., trimmed

*Emendation:*
    2 Holds] Hilds

*Alterations:*
    0.1 Ties.] *added in face 1*
    7 claim] *over* 'flame'
    12 shamèd] *accent added*
## 17 Scat'red] 't' *interl.*

## 20. *Time Laid Low* (TMs)

Typewriter face 1; wove unmarked paper, possibly Columbia University letterhead, 188 x 113 mm., trimmed; on same sheet as No. 59

*Emendation:*
    4 more.] ~∧

## 21. *Two Joys* (TMs)

Typewriter face 1; wove unmarked paper, 168 x 108 mm., trimmed; on same sheet as No. 17

22. *Two Weeks* (TMs)

Typewriter face 5; wove paper marked *Efficiency Bond | A.P. & P. Co.*, four sheets: 268 x 188 mm., 270 x 180 mm., 280 x 193 mm., 276 x 169 mm.

*Emendations:*
24 joy] jpy
63 renounce] renpunce
77 ourselves] pourselves
81 pawnbroker's] pawnbrokers
83 thistles] thsistles
83 cockleburs] cocklecurs
107 from] frm
112 Neither] neither

*Alterations:*
2 guessed] *before x'd-out* 'the things'
3 way,] *comma added in pencil*
7 makes,] *comma added in pencil*
8 then] 'n' *in pencil over* 'm'
23 annoy] *before x'd-out* 'and'
26 it's] *apostrophe added in pencil*
26 eight—] *dash in pencil over semicolon*
36 a] *pencil mark may signal intended del.*
37 moment] *before x'd-out* 'has blent'
42 I am] *interl. in pencil w. caret*
51 against] *before pencil-del.* 'against'
53 stored] *above partly legible word* 'stred'
54 things] *after x'd-out* 'dear'
54 stains] *interl. w. pencil caret and guideline above* 'stains' [*over pencil-del.* 'scars' *above pencil-del.* 'then']
56 th'uneffacèd] *apostrophe after x'd-out* 'e'; *accent added in pencil*
56 scar.] *period in pencil, possibly over other mark*
62 then] *interl. in pencil w. caret*
62 not] 'n' *over* 'N'
68 read,] *comma added in pencil*
80 one] *in pencil over* 'he'
83 of] *before pencil-del.* 'weeds' *and undel. comma*
83 few] *above x'd-out* 'little'
86 in] *before vertical pencil mark for space*
86 today's] *apostrophe added in pencil*
98 on] *in pencil over* 'to'
108 But] *in pencil over* 'As'

## 23. *The Unending Hours* (TMs)

Typewriter face 2; wove paper marked *Hurd's Bank Note Bond,*
201 x 252 mm.

*Emendation:*
    4 prisoned] prisioned

*Alterations:*
    1 ground,] *comma over period*
    6 come] *above* 'come' *over* 'move'
    6 did] *above x'd-out* 'could'
    7 could] *above x'd-out* 'did'
    9 last] *alt. from* 'lest'
    10 —The] *dash inserted in pencil*

## 24. *#When Thou Art Gone* (TMs)

Typewriter face 2; wove paper marked *Hurd's Bank Note Bond,*
125 x 201 mm., torn at bottom

*Emendation:*
    0.1 Thou] THOUE
*Note:* A variant version of this quatrain, entitled "Absence," is
typewritten (face 1) on the same scrap of paper as No. 35.

*Variants:*
    1 mem'ry] memry
    2 Thy presence] And
    2 dream∧] ~;
    4 The] As
    4 ling'ring] *om.*

## 25. #"Across the white of my mind's map" (TMs)

Typewriter face 3; wove unmarked paper, 184 x 225 mm.,
trimmed

*Emendations:*
    1 Across] AAcross
    15 Make] make

*Alterations:*
    2 shines] *alt. from* 'shone'
    5 hot] *interl.*
    5 swollen] *after x'd-out* 'soul's' *and interl. x'd-out* 'fat'
    7 To] *over* 'The'

7 they] *before* x'd-out 'do'
9 my] *alt. from* 'by'
10 Fly] *over* 'Flew'
11 Where] *before* x'd-out 'the sorrows'
11 rains] *interl.*
12 ice] *after* x'd-out 'black'
12 are] *over* 'were'
13 Thus] *over* 'Then'
14 sculptured] *after* x'd-out 'stand'
15 Make] *above* x'd-out 'For'
15 the] *over* 'its'
19 And] *over* 'In'
19 dissolve] *final* 's' *pencil-del.*

## 26. *At the Last* (TMs)

Typewriter face 2; wove paper marked *Hurd's Bank Note Bond,*
164 x 98 mm.

*Emendation:*
4 pleasures.] ~∧

## 27. #*The Child's Garden* (TMs)

Typewriter face 3; lined examination book paper, 132 x 114 mm.,
trimmed

*Emendations:*
0.1 ∧The Child's Garden∧] ''~''.
3 for] frr

*Alterations:*
2 enclosèd] *accent added in pencil*
5 But] 'Bu' *over* 'Fo'
6 barren] *interl.*
7 Docks] 's' *added in pencil*
7 only] *in pencil above pencil-del.* 'sole'
8 closèd] *accent added in pencil*

## 28. "He failed. Though he was strong" (TMs)

Typewriter face 4; wove paper marked *Efficiency Bond,* 180 x 212
mm., torn at top

*Emendations:*
7 success.] ~,
17 cloud.] ~∧

109

*Alterations:*
　2 t' await] 'o' *x'd-out*
　6 streams] *after x'd-out* 'milk'
　7 Too weak] ('T' *in ink over* 't'); *after del.* 'He was', *below x'd-out* 'He was too weak', *above which is x'd-out* 'and in his dreams'
　9 The] *after x'd-out* 'Of' *and del.* 'In silence.'
　10 thorny] *after x'd-out* 'thorny'
　13 Through] *after x'd-out* 'By'
　13 a] *after x'd-out* 'the'
　15 The] *interl.*
　15 thorns] 't' *over* 'T'
　16 Him] *before x'd-out* 'down'
　16 pitfalls;] 's' *over period; semicolon added*
　17 swallowed] *in ink above del.* 'vanished'

## 29. "Last night I stood upon the hill" (TMs)

Typewriter face 4; wove yellow paper marked with two castles, 215 x 215 mm.

*Emendation:*
　26 moonlight's] moonlights

*Alterations* (all alterations except *x'd-out* are in pencil):
　4 stay] *before x'd-out* 'and rest'
　5 stop] *over* 'rest'
　7 oceans,] *comma added*
　8 Poured] *before del.* 'forth'
　8 some] *interl.*
　9+ [*x'd-out line*]] 'With which the firce divisive sun'
　12 Of] *over* 'In'
　12 with which he] *inserted w. guideline from del.* 'he'
　12 begun] *before x'd-out* 'a'
　13 The] *over* 'At'
　13 rose.] *period added*
　14 From . . . swallowed] *inserted w. guideline after del.* 'And fell from sky. All was swallowed'
　15 mercy.] *period over hyphen*
　15 Pleasures] 'P' *over* 'p'
　17 On] *inserted before* 'the'
　17 the] 't' *over* 'T'
## 17 Tho't] *over* 'I too'
　18 In . . . night] *entire line inserted w. guideline to del.* 'quiet bosom' *after undel.* 'In the' *and before undel.* 'of the night'

19 welcome . . . cost] *inserted for del.* '[*illegible word*] welcome paid all' *before undel.* 'the cost'
20 struggles] *inserted w. guideline to del.* 'unrest'
21 Had roused.] *after del.* 'Imposed.'
22 sought] *inserted for del.* 'sent'
23 In] *inserted w. guideline for del.* 'Like'
25 With] *over* 'And'
25 with] *over* 'and'
25 the] *interl.*
26 Through] *over* 'In'
27 Merged] *inserted for del.* 'Melted'
28 By . . . beguiled] *inserted w. guideline for del.* 'Into out-stretched arms *were [*over* 'was'] all beguiled-'
29 slept] *w. guideline below x'd-out* 'lay down'
29 close] *w. guideline below del.* 'together'

## 30. *Little Things* (TMs)

Typewriter face 3; wove unmarked paper, 180 x 252 mm.

*Emendations:*
5 cherubim] cherumbim
21 My] my
21 cockrel's] cockrel'

*Alterations:*
10 minds] *above x'd-out* 'ears'
11 me,] *comma added*
15 And] *in ink over* 'I'
16 beside;] *semicolon alt. in ink from colon*
30 be",] *comma added*
32 little] *after del.* 'loving'
32 foolish] *interl. in ink w. caret*

## 31. "Long time lay the world level and open" (TMs)

Typewriter face 1; wove unmarked paper, 196 x 165 mm., trimmed

*Emendation:*
16 flow.] ~∧

*Alterations:*
3 by] *above x'd-out* 'of'
5 idle] *above x'd-out* 'swolln'
6 to one] *above x'd-out* 'together'

111

7 Not . . . ill] *above x'd-out* 'Awaiting as startled mice approach of ill'
11 Passed] 'sed' *above x'd-out* 't'
12 Plenitude] ('P' *over* 'p'); *after x'd-out* 'Since'
12 the same as] *above x'd-out* 'was like'
12 lack of] *interl.*
14 moments,] *before x'd-out* 'one from each and all' *above which is* 'marking one ['out' *x'd-out*] from all,'

## 32. *Mine Own Body* (TMs)

Typewriter face 1; wove unmarked paper sealed in plastic, possibly Columbia University letterhead, 173 x 134 mm.

*Emendations:*

3 toppling] topplings
8 were] wre
8 ashes] aahes
8 flames'] ~ ∧
15 unmeaning] unmeanings

*Alterations:*

9 life;] *semicolon added*
10+ [stanza break]] *guideline for stanza break*
12 great] *ink-inserted w. guideline from del.* 'long'
13 Long] *in ink over* 'Had'
18 mine] *before x'd-out* 'house'
20 faring] *before del.* 'abroad'
22 war's] "s' *in ink*
22 tempestuous lot.] *in ink below del.* 'tumultuous fraught.'

## 33. *My Fever* (TMs)

Typewriter face 3; wove unmarked paper, 158 x 242 mm., trimmed

*Alterations:*

1 vase] 'e' *in ink over* 'e,'
6 Where] 'Wh' *over* 'Of'
7 thoughts,] 's,' *in ink*
7 mixèd] *accent added*
12 body,] *comma added*
12 blent,] *comma added*
16 Boundless] *final* 'ly' *del.*

## 34. ## "My mind is but a gutt'ring candle dip" (MS)

Wove paper marked *W.S. & B. Paragon Linen / Made in U.S.A.*, Columbia University letterhead, 176 x 171 mm.; on same sheet as No. 12

*Emendation:*
    5 Lord.] ~ ∧

*Alterations:*
    2 the] *interl.*
    2 doth blow] *above del. illegible word*
    5 the] *interl. w. caret*

## 35. *My Road* (TMs)

Typewriter face 1; wove unmarked paper, 151 x 131 mm.; on same sheet as No. 24

*Emendation:*
    4 That] Tha

## 36. "Not now thy scourging rod" (TMs)

Typewriter face 1, carbon copy; wove unmarked paper, 206 x 235 mm.

*Emendations:*
    5 withhold] withold
    6 infinite] infinte
    22 all] All

*Alterations:*
    22 Yet] *in ink before* 'All'
    22 long] *before del.* 'shall'
    22 shall] *alt. in ink from* 'still'
*Note:* Dewey's pencil note in upper left-hand corner, 'Complete'.

## 37. "Not wrinkled, shrivelled, grey" (TMs)

Typewriter face 3; wove unmarked paper, 173 x 122 mm.

*Emendation:*
    11 Year] year

*Alterations:*
    1+ [*x'd-out line*]] 'Goesby the old year'
    4 with] *after del.* 'but'
    6 In] *over* 'As'

113

7 day,] *comma added*
9 bunchèd] *accent added*
11 is] *before partly x'd-out* 'the'
12 As] ('A' *in ink over* 'a'); *after del.* 'A boy'

## 38. #*Pulse in an Earthen Jar* (TMs)

Typewriter face 5; wove unmarked paper, 181 x 236 mm., trimmed

*Emendations:*

0.1 Pulse in an Earthen Jar] Pulse in an earthern jar.
2 potter's] potters'
8 was once a] was once was a
19 summer's] summers'

*Alterations:*

12 from] *alt. from* 'of'
13 ancestors] *alt. from* 'ancestry'
13 were] *above x'd-out* 'was'
13 cattle] *before x'd-out* 'too.'

*Note:* The content and language of this poem cast some doubt on Dewey's authorship of it. The typewriter face is that of Evelyn Dewey's machine, on which only three poems were typed—this one, *Two Weeks,* and *To Death.* The typewriting pattern seems to be Dewey's, but the referent of the italic *"he"* (one of only three italicized words in the poems) is not clear, nor is it possible to interpret the meaning of the poem in terms of Dewey's life or thought. The key expression, "Well he was born of his mother / And I of mine, / And both of a long long line," does also appear in No. 72, *Education,* as "My fathers and my fathers' fathers arrayed / In long receding generations."

At the same time, Anzia Yezierska has a similar expression in *All I Could Never Be,* "the long line of men who made her father" (p. 215), and a case might be made for her having written the poem if the "pulse in an earthen jar" is interpreted as a metaphor for Yezierska herself—a vital force enclosed in clay, the "irregular groove" as her "faults," and "the king" as a bitter reference to Dewey and the differences between their lives. With this interpretation and with authorship attributed to her, the meaning of the poem—particularly the last stanza—may become clearer.

## 39. *Respite* (TMs)

Typewriter face 2; wove paper marked *Hurd's / Bank Note / Bond,* 174 x 73 mm.

*Alterations:*
>   1 sand] 's' *over and also above* 'l'
>   2 deep] 'er' *x'd-out*

## 40. *Romance* (TMs)

Typewriter face 4; wove unmarked paper, two sheets, both trimmed: 145 x 265 mm., 146 x 261 mm.

*Emendations:*
>   4 tense] Tense
>  16 shook] skook
>  18 And] and
>  27 afield] afiled
>  41 twelve] tewelve
>  45 He] he
>  47 Swore] Sore

*Alterations:*
>   1 springily] *alt. from* 'springy'
>  11 in] *after x'd-out* 'he'
>  16 Again] 'A' *over* 'S'
>  34 somehow,] *before x'd-out* 'the'
>  51 emptiness,] *comma added in pencil*
>  51 he] 'h' *over* 'H' *in pencil*
>  51 swore.] *period over comma in pencil*
>  53 into] *before x'd-out* 'the'

## 41. "That frail ship I load with limitless freight" (TMs)

Typewriter face 1; wove paper marked *W.S. & B. Paragon Linen / Made in U.S.A.,* Columbia University letterhead, 188 x 236 mm., trimmed

*Alterations:*
>   1 That] *above x'd-out* 'Yonder'
>  13 Commerce] ('C' *over* 'c'); *after x'd-out* 'In'

## 42. "Tho all the rhymes were long since rhymed" (TMs)

Typewriter face 3; laid paper marked *Treasury Linen,* chains 25 mm. apart, 187 x 109 mm., trimmed

*Alterations:*
>   3 joy] (*in face 1*); *above x'd-out* 'love'
>   5 bodies] *alt. from* 'babies'
>   6 what's] (*in face 1*); *above x'd-out* 'the'
>   8 fresh] (*in face 1*); *above x'd-out* 'newer'

*Note:* At bottom of sheet upside down, appears the following in face 4: '35 / the *way* of activity called for.'

43. *To Conscience* (TMs)

Typewriter face 3; laid paper marked *Treasury Linen*, chains 25 mm. apart, 187 x 215 mm.

*Emendations:*
    1 on!] ~$_\wedge$
    1 and] &
    2 $_\wedge$Evil] "~
    2 forces."] ~$_{\wedge\wedge}$
    4 embriared;] ~.
    5 courses.] ~;
    7 Toiled] toiled
    12 Shall . . . pleasure] *del.*
    13 strain?] ~,
    17 stain.] ~,

*Alterations:*

    0.1 To Conscience] *ink-inserted*
    #1 on!] *before del.* ' "you say'
    1 Combat] ('C' *over* 'c'); *in ink after inserted then del.* 'In'
    #1 and] *inserted and interl. in ink after* 'Combat'
    1 conquer] *inserted in ink over ink* 'must'
    2+ [*del. line*]] 'That press to have their way".'
    3 I] *after del.* 'But'
    3 tired$_\wedge$] *semicolon del.*
    4 Of this] *in ink above del.* 'I shall turn from'
    #4–5 Of . . . courses.] *lines reversed by ink guideline*
    6 got] *after del.* 'have'
    #7 Toiled] *after del.* 'Have'
    9 and] *before del.* 'een'
    9 take their] *in ink over* 'turn to'
    10 stern] *in ink over illegible word*
    11 thy] *in ink below del.* 'unceasing'
    11 endless] *in ink above del.* 'unceasing'; *after ink interl. then del.* 'this'
    #13 strain?] *before x'd-out* 'Never sail a sea of azure'
    14 Let me] *in ink over* 'Never'
    15 Wave . . . pleasure] *added*
    16 Turn from] *in ink over* 'But alays'
    16 treading] 'ing' *added*

17+ [*del. lines*]] 'While idly drunk my foe *but [*in ink over* 'idly'] mocks? / This life of work is not worth while;'

18 Give] *above undel.* 'Give'

21+ [*del. line*]] 'I now must do but as I please.'

22 conscience,] *comma added*

22 cease] *before del.* 'then'

*Note 1:* In the right margin: 'upon / son / ton / wan / ocur / [*illegible word*] / defer / Fight on! / Fight on! Bestir! / Resume the battle.'

*Note 2:* Line 12, deleted in ink on the TMs, has been restored to complete the rhyme scheme and meaning of the stanza, on the assumption that Dewey either deleted unintentionally, or, if intentionally, failed to insert a substitute line.

44. *To Death* (TMs)

Typewriter face 5; wove unmarked paper, 182 x 258 mm., trimmed

45. "To us you came from out of dark" (TMs)

Typewriter face 3; lined notebook paper, 171 x 145 mm., slanting to 128 mm., torn at bottom

*Emendations:*

8 ours] our

12 strove] srove

12 touch.] ~ ∧

*Alterations:*

1 from] *interl. in ink*

1 dark] *after del.* 'the'

2 To] ('T' *in ink over* 't'); *after del.* 'As' *and undel.* 'if'

3 that] *in ink over* 'his' *after del.* 'so soon'

4 ours] 's' *added*

4 lent] *after del.* 'to us'

6 Brightest] 'est' *in pencil over ink* 'ness' *over illegible letters*

6 of] *in ink over* 'the' *after del.* 'of all'

7 life] *alt. from* 'lives'

7 sweet] *before del.* 'and clean'

9 dwelt—] *dash added*

10 much?] *question mark added*

11 Again] ('A' *in ink over* 'a'); *after del.* 'That'

11 a] *in ink over* 'the'

11 dying] *above x'd-out* 'failing'

12 vainly] *after pencil-del.* 'outstretched'

117

13–14 And . . . loan.] *pencil-del.* 'And hold our own / Ah brave
bright soul / God's blessed loan. / [*illegible word*] stole'
*Note:* The two new final lines needed to complete this sonnet
may have been torn off the bottom of the ragged sheet of paper
on which the poem appears. Lacking any substitute, the pencil-
deleted lines have been restored.

46. *Two Births* (TMs)

Typewriter face 1; wove unmarked paper, 193 x 238 mm.,
trimmed

*Emendations:*
15 used] useed
20 shall] shal

*Alteration:*
3 youth] 'y' *over* 'Y'

47. *Creation* (TMs)

Typewriter face 1; wove unmarked paper, two complete TMss,
ribbon: R, and carbon: C
R: p. 1, 210 x 270 mm.; p. 2, 213 x 278 mm.; p. 3, 203 x 238
mm.
C: p. 1, 188 x 277 mm.; p. 2, 188 x 278 mm.; p. 3, 190 x 217
mm.
Copy-text is C: carbon copy of TMs, which has only Dewey's
own alterations.

*Variants:*
2 kiss] kisses
4 unchanging∧] ~, (*comma added in ink*)
13 lusts—] ~,
14 To] Mad to
16 shrank; then] shrank. Then (*period and 'T' in ink*)
21 Imaged] Conceiving
21 woe to] woe yet to
21 future born] born
24 broke] break
38 oer charged] (*vertical mark for space*); oercharged
50 Should] Might

*Emendations:*
4 unchanging,] R; ~∧
17 unknown] unkown
19 maddened] maddenned
27 obscene] obseene

118

28 Time's] time's
36 night's] nights
37 Time] time
## 38 o'ercharged] R; oer charged
44 whence] whene
46 clashing] clasing
49 marbled] marbles
55 Time's] time's
57 Eternity] eternity

*Alterations:*
   2 kiss] *final 'es' del.*
  13 Life] *'L' over 'l'*
  13 lusts—] *dash in ink over comma*
  14 To] *('T' over 't'); after del. 'Mad'*
  14 world's] *'wo' over 'th'*
  16 shrank;] *semicolon added*
  21 Imaged] *in ink above del. 'Conceiving'*
  21 woe] *before del. 'yet' and 'not' interl. in ink then del.*
  21 future] *interl. in ink w. caret*
  24 broke] *alt. from 'break'*
  24+ [*del. line*]] 'While far fields of unfencèd wand'ring foam'
  34 through] *interl.*
  38 Felt] *before x'd-out 'issue'*
  42 changing] *above x'd-out 'new'*
  49 red—] *dash added*
  50 Should] *in ink above del. 'Might'*
  53 feeble] *in ink above del. 'tender'*
  57 And] *in ink over 'As'*
*Note:* Critical comments in Alice Dewey's hand appear on ribbon copy. Dewey's typewritten and handwritten corrections are on both R and C. No. 57 is a variant of Section I; No. 56 is a variant of the start of Section II.


48. "Dear moon and stars, and dearer yet" (TMs)

Typewriter face 4; wove paper marked *Efficiency Bond,* 166 x 84 mm., torn at top

*Alterations:*
  5 lights] *after x'd-out 'that'*
  6 shadows] *after x'd-out 'baby'*


49. "Earth-born dust rising in the air" (TMs)

Typewriter face 1; wove paper, 190 x 135 mm., sealed in plastic

*Alterations:*

    1 rising] (*alt. from* 'risen'); *after del.* 'quiet'
    4 dust] *interl. after x'd-out* 'earth'
    4 motes] *after x'd-out* 'sun'
    5 eager] *interl.*
    5 drank] *after x'd-out* 'eager'
    5 earthen] *above x'd-out* 'mellow'
    6 Full] *after x'd-out* 'Of earth'
##6 to gold'n rim of] ('t' *over* 'T'); *above x'd-out* 'of'
    7 dim hazy] *above x'd-out* 'wild magic'
    9 Whereby] *above x'd-out* 'Of magic, whence'
    9 magic] *interl.*
    11 So that] *ink-inserted*
    11 phantom things] *interl. w. caret and guideline after x'd-out* 'seen things' *which is above del.* 'To make' *and x'd-out* 'objects'
    11 stood] *alt. from* 'stand'

## 50. "Fair flowers grow in my garden ground" (TMs)

Typewriter face 4; wove paper marked *Efficiency Bond,* 174 x 205 mm., torn at top

*Alterations:*

    7 And] *in ink over* 'While'
    7 quick] *interl. w. caret*
##8 flow'r's] 'e' *del.*
    9 a] *interl. w. caret*
    9 lazy] *alt. in ink from* 'hazy'
    10 perfumes] (*final* 's' *added*); *after del.* 'sweet'
    10 that] *interl. in ink w. caret*
    10 lang'rous] 'o' *del.; possible ink apostrophe*
    11 from] *in pencil above x'd-out* 'with'
    11 of its daughter] *above x'd-out* 'from the coming'
    14 Thou] 'T' *in pencil over* 't'; *two illegible letters pencil-del. at end*
    14+ [*x'd-out line*]] 'their discordant shock, where ['the' *interl., x'd-out*] roses bloom'
    16 careless] *alt. from* 'thoughtless'
    18 wc] *alt. in ink from* 'be'

## 51. *A Fallow Field* (TMs)

Typewriter face 3; wove unmarked paper, 142 x 108 mm., trimmed; on same sheet as No. 55

*Alterations:*

  1 of] *in pencil over* 'like'

  1 sprightly] *in pencil above pencil-del.* 'stately'

  2 In daring mood] *in pencil below pencil-del.* 'In gathered groups'

  2 beck] *below x'd-out* 'wave'

  3 bonnets'] 's" *in pencil over x'd-out* 'ed'

  3 wild] *in pencil above pencil-del.* 'queer'

  3+ [*x'd-out line*]] 'In a strange land where no'

  4 meek] *in pencil below pencil-del.* 'well'

## 52. "From my glance backward sent recedes" (TMs)

Typewriter face 1; wove unmarked paper, 167 x 271 mm., badly torn at top and left side

*Emendations:*

  2 onward] onwards

  12 rhythmic] rythmic

  15 man] men

  18 own] oon

  22 trees] tress

*Alterations:*

  1 From] *over* 'Tp'

  1 glance backward sent recedes,] (*comma added*); *w. caret above del.* 'backward looking glance recedes'; 'sent' *del. after* 'glance', *ink interl. w. caret*

  2 from] *after x'd-out* 'viewed'

  4 sand-blown] 'wind blown with sand' *interl., del.*

  4 of] *in ink over* 'by'

  7 Its] *in ink over* 'By'

  7 rim,] *comma added*

  7+ [*x'd-out line*]] 'Meadows miraged by watry meres'

  8 gay] *moved w. guideline from after* 'dance'

  9 seen⋀] *comma x'd-out*

  11 which] *in ink w. caret above del.* 'that'

  18 Within] *in ink w. caret above del.* 'As by'

  18 hearts] 's' *added*

##18 utter'd] *after del.* 'inner'

  21 surging] *alt. in ink from* 'urgent'

  22 joys,] *comma added*

  22 At] *in ink over* 'On'

  22 glad] *after x'd-out* 'earth with'

  23 Of] *in ink w. caret above del.* 'With'

  23 arms,] *comma added*

26 ⌊*illegible word*⌋] *in ink over* 'While'
26 flashing] 'ing' *interl. in ink w. caret*

## 53. *In the Country* (TMs)

Typewriter face 4; wove paper marked *Efficiency Bond,* 182 x 187 mm.

*Alterations:*
10 tender] *interl. w. caret*
10 longing] *after x'd-out* 'tender'
15 Within] 'in' *interl. w. caret*
16 splendor] *after del.* 'the'
19 th'] 'e' *x'd-out*

## 54. *Indian Summer at the Farm* (TMs)

Typewriter face 1; wove paper marked *W.S. & B. Paragon / Made in U.S.A.,* Columbia University Department of Philosophy letterhead, 175 x 267 mm., trimmed

*Alterations*
0.1 at] *over* 'on'
3 O'ει] *apostrophe and* 'e' *in ink over* 'u'
12 gold] *after x'd-out* 'dull an'
20 time's] *in ink below del.* 'day's'

## 55. *A Journey* (TMs)

Typewriter face 1; wove unmarked paper, 142 x 108 mm., trimmed; on same sheet as No. 51

## 56. "Life blithe in lusty action restless and rude" (TMs)

Typewriter face 1; wove unmarked paper, 151 x 115 mm.

*Emendations:*
3 to do] to to do
5 means] menas

*Alterations:*
1 restless] *after x'd-out* 'a'
2 by] 'y' *over* 'ıı'
2 end] *after x'd-out* 'intent'
3 hurrying] *interl.*
3 come,] *before x'd-out* 'and'
3 go] *after x'd-out* 'pass'
4 touch] *after x'd-out* 'move and change'

*Note:* These lines are a variant part of Section II of No. 47; above them are the trial lines: 'a guest *of [*over* 'in'] the savage hostelry of pain / ['Oer' *x'd-out*] Flooding ['F' *over* 'f'] the sky's pent wieir / Poured firce *['the' *x'd-out*] black [*above x'd-out* 'floods of'] ['floods' *x'd-out*] torrents straight and sheer / From the swollen sky's oerflooded weir / Fierce poured *the [*below x'd-out* 'black'] torrents straight and sheer'.

57. "Like fogs from some black cave of mournful night" (TMs)

Typewriter face 1; wove unmarked paper, 195 x 199 mm., trimmed

*Emendation:*
16+ [*om.*]] II.

*Alterations:*
2 uncertain] *after del.* 'from'
2 its] *interl. in ink*
3 beaches—] *dash over comma*
5 by the] *in ink over* 'of light'
5 sun's] *before del.* 'sharp' *and ink-interl. del.* 'steely' *w. caret and guideline to question mark*
5 plowshare—] *dash over comma*
6 trod] *interl. in ink before interl.* '['stirred' *del.*] but by' *above x'd-out* 'trod only by' ['the' *del.*]
7 Unchanging . . . grey] *above del.* 'Clothed in unchanging garb of pallid grey,'
8 purposes unthought] *above x'd-out* 'unboded doo unboded dooms'
9 Deeds . . . unboded.] *above x'd-out* 'Far purposes unthought and deeds undone, / Set in secret patterns of clouded tissue. / [*stanza break*] Passive she waited thru becalmèd years'
9 unfelt] *after del.* 'Fears unfelt dooms unboded.'
11 burdened] *after x'd-out* 'weighted'
14 unconscious] *after x'd-out* 'moved on'
15 Moved] ('M' *over* 'm'); *after x'd-out* 'With itself'
15 on] *interl.*
16 torp'r] "r' *in ink over* 'or'
16 of] *interl.*
*Note:* This poem is a variant version of the first stanza of No. 47.

58. *A Moment and a Time* (TMs)

Typewriter face 1; wove unmarked paper, 180 x 238 mm., trimmed

*Emendations:*
>     3  twilight's] twilights'
>     5  moment's] moments
>     6  silence's] slience's
>    13  their] thier
>    18  trumpet's] trumpets
>    20  wingèd] winged
>    21  rhythmic] rythmic

*Alterations:*
>  0.1+ [*undel. false start under title*]] 'Close by the clouds'
>     1  up] *interl. w. caret*
>     2  feet] *above x'd-out* 'day'
>     4  breathless] *after x'd-out* 'brathless'
>     6  In] *above x'd-out* 'From out'
>     7  arrested] *after x'd-out* 'exchanged'
>     7  by . . . hesitation] *above x'd-out* 'took each its lasting station'
>     8  Like] *after x'd-out* 'Were'
>     8  in] *final* 't' *x'd-out*
>    18  if by] *above x'd-out* 'when the'
>    19  As] *over* 'So'
>    21  shapes] *above x'd-out* 'forms,'

59. *The Mountain's Hour* (TMs)

Typewriter face 1; wove unmarked paper, possibly Columbia University letterhead, 188 x 113 mm., trimmed; on same sheet as No. 20.

*Alteration:*
>     3  ceaseless] 'ess' *above* 'ing'

60. "Now night, mother soul, broods the weary hours" (TMs)

Typewriter face 3; wove unmarked paper, 184 x 252 mm., trimmed on left

*Alterations:*
>     1  night,] *final* 's' *pencil-del.; comma added in pencil*
>     1  soul,] *comma added in pencil*
>     4  sharp] *above x'd-out* 'bright'

10 of] *before two illegible x'd-out and pencil-del. letters*
10 unwingèd vict'ry] *accent and apostrophe added in pencil*
12 presence;] *semicolon added in pencil*
13 And] *w. pencil caret above pencil-del.* 'Till'
13 were] *after pencil-del.* 'they'
13 together] *w. pencil caret above x'd-out* 'with'
13 within] *after pencil-del.* 'in peace'
20 own,] *comma added in pencil*
22 severed] *moved w. pencil guideline from before* 'spirits'
22 men] 'e' *in pencil over* 'a'
23 fretful] *interl. w. pencil caret*
24 Wond'ring] *pencil apostrophe above pencil-del.* 'e'
24 the] *before x'd-out* 'wondrous'
24 enduring] *interl. w. pencil caret*

## 61. *Renewal* (TMs)

Typewriter face 3, title in ink; laid paper marked *Treasury Linen,* chains 25 mm. apart, 151 x 215 mm.

*Alteration:*
    0.1 Renewal] *ink-inserted*

## 62. "The rope is cut, the anchor falls" (TMs)

Typewriter face 4; wove paper marked *P. & P. Co.* (first line, *Efficiency Bond* cut off) (second line 'A' cut off?), 179 x 268 mm., trimmed

*Emendations:*
    20 ship.] ~,
    23 screeching] scre dhing

*Alterations:*
    9 now] *interl.*
    10 waste] *after x'd-out* 'stuff'
    22 Knocks.] *period over comma*

## 63. *America* (TMs)

Typewriter face 3; wove unmarked paper, 158 x 220 mm., trimmed

*Emendations:*
    1 wide] wides
    14 shawls] sha ls

*Alteration:*
    2 in,] *before x'd-out* 'and still they hurrying come'

### 64. "And high God on his throne" (TMs)

Typewriter face 3; wove unmarked paper, 174 x 141 mm., trimmed

*Emendations:*
    4 Making] making
    6 off] nff
    9 little] littl

*Alterations:*
    2 throne] *after x'd-out* 'remote'
    2 rocking] *interl.*
    7 piercing] *after x'd-out* 'and'
    8 last] *interl.*
    10 [*x'd-out word*]] 'fate' *inserted, x'd-out before* 'Saints'
    10 blame] *after x'd-out* 'shame' *and pencil-del.* 'self'
    11 blame] *over* 'shame'
    12 While] *in ink above del.* 'As if'
    12 babies] 'ies' *in ink over* 'es'
    12 cried] *over* 'called'
    12 shame.] *after x'd-out* 'blame.'

### 65. "And shall we shut the door" (TMss)

TMs[1] Typewriter face 4; wove paper marked *Efficiency Bond*, 211 x 280 mm., trimmed
TMs[2] Typewriter face 6; laid unmarked paper, chains 25 mm. apart, 147 x 132 mm.
Copy-text is TMs[1]

*Variants:*
    9 coals,] *ink comma over period*
    9 shall] 's' *in ink over* 'S'

### 66. "And the lad eager replied: No sir, not a God damned Word" (TMs)

Typewriter face 3; wove unmarked paper, 212 x 242 mm., trimmed

*Emendations:*

    1 And] Znd

    1 replied:] ~ ;

    4 man's] mans

    5 And] Snd

    5 which] whi h

    5 his] hs

    6 spirit's] spirits

*Alterations:*

    1 lad] *after x'd-out* 'eager'

    1 eager] *interl.*

    2 put] *above x'd-out* 'let'

    2 me] *before x'd-out* 'go'

    2+ [x'd-out line]] 'A big boy lie you, a man in size and strength'

    3 old] *after x'd-out* 'worn'

    3 hearing] *above x'd-out* 'catching God s'

    3+ [*line inserted then x'd-out*]] 'Tho worn with his long teaching the old'

    4 heart] *before x'd-out* 'the divine message'

    7 hath] *above x'd-out* 'is'

*Note:* This fragment is at the bottom of the page, immediately preceded by the following four trial lines: 'While ters thethe / And through the tears *with which [*above x'd-out* 'that'] th['e' x'd-out] old mans eyes *were [*interl.* ('his ears' *inserted undel.*]] blurred / He saw ['again descending' *x'd-out*] the dove of ['holy' *x'd-out*] spirit descend *holy dove [*interl.*] qiuck [*after x'd-out* 'again'] / As it hath from the *begiining ['be' *interl.*] and shall *untill ['un' *interl.*] the end'.

At the top of this sheet are two sets of lines, probably not intended as part of the poem started below: 'For having the money they paid the taxes / And with schooling ungrateful ambition waxes / For sine they had the money and the real estate / For since they had the money ['they' *x'd-out*] grudging ['they' *interl.*] paid ['had to pay' *interl.*] the scant school tax / To dole learning to Hun ['and pole' *x'd-out*] and Fin at cheapest rate / Grumbling least by learning ambution ungrateful mig ['might wax' *inserted*]'.

In the left margin appear one above the other these words: 'word / bird / occurd / blurd / gird / heard / sirrred / averred'.

## 67. "Because the plan of world is dim and blurred" (TMs)

Typewriter face 1; wove unmarked paper, 172 x 240 mm., trimmed

*Emendations:*
>     7 Shall] Sahll
>     8 Because] Beacuse

*Alterations:*
>     2 wise] *interl.*
>     9 Stoic] 'S' *over* 's'
>     12 briar] *after del.* 'wild'
>     17 accident,] *comma in ink over dash*
>     18 Whose] *in ink over* 'Its'

*Note:* At the foot of the page appears the word 'necessity' some eight lines above the following couplet that was probably being revised to complete the second stanza and which has been used here to complete the clear text: 'Not ['t *above* 'w'] while racing rivers run to sea / Bearing on  heir bosom ['their' *x'd-out*] this unbound me.'

## 68. *Borrowed* (TMs)

Typewriter face 1; wove unmarked paper, 145 x 110 mm.

*Emendations:*
>     4 station.] ~ ∧
>     8 onward] ownward
>     11 yet] Yet

*Alterations:*
>     11 Knows] 'K' *in ink over* 'k'
>    # 11 yet] *moved by ink guideline and caret from before* 'Knows'
>     11 liberty:—] ':—' *in ink over period*
>     16 It] *final* 's' *del.*

## 69. *Brave Things* (TMs)

Typewriter face 3; wove unmarked paper, 188 x 256 mm., trimmed

*Emendation:*
>     9 unknown] unkniwn

*Alterations:*
>     5 depths] ('s' *in ink); after del.* 'depe'
>     8 on] 'n' *in ink over* 'f'
>     12 as] *in ink below del.* 'but'

## 70. *But—* (TMs)

Typewriter face 1; wove unmarked paper, 195 x 245 mm., trimmed

*Emendation:*
>9 domed] domes

*Alterations:*
>4 fang] 'f' *over* 'p'
>15 sickened] 'ened' *inserted in pencil w. guideline*

## 71. *Duplicity* (TMs)

Typewriter face 1; wove unmarked paper, 158 x 128 mm., trimmed

*Emendations:*
>10 stern-lipped] sternₐlippied
>14 both] Both

*Alterations:*
>8 Sending her] *in pencil above pencil-del.* 'Both point me'
>10 speaks] *alt. in pencil from* 'spake'
>12 sings] *alt. in pencil from* 'sang'
>13 Dew-steeped] *hyphen added in pencil*
>13 rose afire] *in pencil after pencil-del.* 'fire'

## 72. *Education* (TMs)

Typewriter face 3; wove unmarked paper, three sheets: 185 x 260 mm., 174 x 265 mm., 185 x 196 mm., all trimmed

*Emendations:*
>3 buzzings] Buzzings
>30 knew] kn w
>31 afraid] wfraid
>35 you] ymu
>44 first I] firstl
>45 Properly] Prpoerly
>56 Lest] *illegible alt.*
>68 Stammering] stammering

*Alterations:*
>2 us] 'u' *over* 'a'
>2 wallₐ] *comma x'd-out*
>4 i'] *alt. from* 'in'
>4 the] *over x'd-out illegible word*
>4+ [x'd-out line]] 'The deafened me in confusion'
>5 That] 'at' *over* 'ey'
>5 I was captured] *above x'd-out* 'captured me'; 'captured' *in pencil over* 'taken'
>6 outward things] *above x'd-out* 'important things'

  6 clear;] *semicolon in pencil over period*
  7 about] *after pencil-del.* 'all'
  8 grown] *after pencil-del.* 'many'
  8 said,] ('s' *in pencil over comma); added in pencil*
10 Urging] *before pencil-del.* 'me'
11 Until] *alt. in pencil from* 'Till'
12 Yet,] *comma added in pencil*
15 Those] ('T' *over* 't'); *after x'd-out* 'In'
16 said . . . is] *in pencil over* 'they said it was'
17 you] *in pencil over* 'I'
17 lid] *after x'd-out* 'the'
18 Lifts] *alt. in pencil from* 'lifted'; *after pencil-del.* 'Was'
18 the] *in pencil above x'd-out and pencil-del.* 'the'
18 things] *in pencil over* 'books'
19 is] *in pencil over* 'was'
19 to be] *interl.*
20 you] *in pencil over* 'i'
21 Before the] *over x'd-out* '*UnTil ['T' *over* 't'] the emty'
21 your] *in pencil over* 'my' *above x'd-out* 'my'
21 be] *in pencil over* 'oer' *above pencil-del.* 'were'
##21 o'erdecked] 'oe'r' *in pencil above* 'decked'
22 With stiff] *inserted before x'd-out* 'With'
23 Brought] *in pencil below pencil-del.* 'Taken'
23 from] *partly over undel.* 'Of'
26 that] *in pencil over* 'it'
27 raise] 'rai' *over* 'lif'
27 'bove] *apostrophe in pencil over* 'a'
29 Gaze] *above x'd-out* 'Look'
32 nor] 'n' *in pencil*
32+ [x'd-out line]] 'To presume upon a right'
33 one] *over* 'me'
33 dare to claim] *above x'd-out* 'presume upon'
33 a] *in pencil over* 'a'
34 you] *over* 'thee'
34 and] *in pencil over* 'nor'
34 pretend] *over* 'presume'; *after x'd-out* 'suppose'
35 descend] *after pencil-del.* 'con'; *below x'd-out* 'send'
38 always] *after x'd-out* 'tend'
42 Above . . . all.] *in pencil below pencil-del.* 'Whom *well
    [*above x'd-out* 'in secret'] I knew to be my all.'
44 taught] *before x'd-out* 'before'
44 must] *after undel.* 'first' *partly over* 'that I' *above which is*
    'firstl'
47 And that] *above x'd-out* 'In short'
48 patient] *above* 'must' *and x'd-out* 'pre'

48 must] *in pencil w. guideline above x'd-out* 'paring'

49 The] 'e' *in pencil over apostrophe*

49 wild and free] *in pencil w. caret above pencil-del.* 'absorb-ing'

50 frank] *in pencil above x'd-out* 'loving'

50 converse] *above x'd-out* 'speech'

#56 Lest] *under illegible pencil correction*

56 may] *in pencil over* 'should'

57 knew,] *comma added in pencil*

57+ [x'd-out line]] 'You were their preparations foe'

58 so.] *period in pencil over other mark*

58+ [*pencil-del. lines*]] 'Since [*above x'd-out* 'And that'] your only censure / was for him who would not venture.'

60 yet] *in pencil over* 'still'

62 medium] *after pencil-del.* 'the'

64 hide] *after x'd-out* 'cowring'

65 change] (*final* 'd' *pencil-del.*); *after pencil-del.* 'have'

65 by] *over* 'in'

69 us] *above x'd-out* 'those'

70 we] *above x'd-out* 'they'

71 safe,—] *dash over* 'ly'; *comma added in pencil*


## 73. *Forgetfulness* (TMs)

Typewriter face 3; wove unmarked paper, 188 x 133 mm., trimmed

*Emendation:*

3 rhythmic] rythmic

*Alterations:*

3 depths] *after x'd-out* 'gulfs od tim'

7 pleas] *final* 'e' *pencil-del.*

7 murmured,] *comma added in pencil*

9 wails'] 'w' *in pencil over illegible letter*

9 vanquisher] *after pencil-del.* 'sole'

10 thy] *in pencil above pencil-del. illegible word*

10 ush'ring] *apostrophe in pencil above pencil-del.* 'e'

11 outstretchèd] *accent added in pencil*

12 Mother] *after pencil-del.* 'dear'; 'the' *inserted in pencil then del. below* 'dear'


## 74. #"Heaven and ground, smooth sky and shore" (MS)

Wove yellowed paper marked *Empire / USA / Bond*, 213 x 275 mm.

131

*Emendations:*
> 1(2) and] &
> 4 and die.] & ~ ∧
> 9(2) and] &
> 15 and] &
> 20 and] &
> 20 kind.] ~ —

*Alterations:*
> 4 the] *over* 'a'
> 5 road] *above del.* 'broad'
> 8+ [*stanza break*]] *guideline to separate stanzas*
> 10+ [*del. line partly legible*]] 'Oer [*illegible word*] *foolish ['of the' *interl.*] space that has no edge'
> ## 11 O'er] *over* 'over'
> 11 a] *above del.* 'the'
> 11 no] *interl.*
> 18 puny] *above del.* 'futile'
> #20 both . . . kind.] *above del.* 'each to his kind.'

*Note:* In upper right hand part of sheet appear the lines: 'Within his garret the fluttered bat / May fix his home firm & pat / Ensconced in tunnel the sleek mole / [*stanza space*] / Let covered mole and garret bat stick fast / Fix the limits *let [*interl.*] him [*alt. from* 'he'] who will / *Whether in cellar [*w. guideline to precede the following del. lines* 'Dig *down [*interl.*] for cellar heave up a hill / Not fast to this one [*illegible word*] hard at that / A tunnell'] mole or garret bat / [*illegible word inserted*]'.

### 75. #"Language, fourth dimension of the mind" (TMs)

Typewriter face 1; wove unmarked paper, 192 x 261 mm., trimmed

*Emendations:*
> 1 Language] language
> 2 curled] culr;d
> 7 sooth] soooth
> 8 i'] in
> 8 crops] Crops
> 9 Men's] Mens
> 12 Stones] stones
> 19 may] doth may
> 21 bequeathed] bequathed
> 22 By] 'y' x'd-out
> 22 salvage] savage
> 24 mage.] ~ ∧

*Alterations:*

      3 turn] *interl.*

      3 unbroken] *before x'd-out* 'turn'

   # 8 growing . . . crops] *above x'd-out* 'in topping fields'

      9 Simples] *before x'd-out* 'both'

  # 12 Stones] *after x'd-out* 'Blind' *and interl. x'd-out* 'Dumb'

    12 to] *interl.*

    12 t'] *interl.*

    13 By . . . revive;] *in right margin to replace undel.* 'By [*over* 'In'] *magic of [interl.] words things *past [*above x'd-out* 'longest'] things [*above x'd-out* 'dead'] revive;'

   13+ [*x'd-out lines*]] 'Frailest things [*interl.* 'braced' *x'd-out*] next firm revive / Frail feeble thots are kept alive / So regaining a lost potency'

    14 To] *above x'd-out* 'And'

    15 Like] *above x'd-out* 'Of'

    15 decay of] *interl. after interl. x'd-out* 'in spite of'

    16 They] *above x'd-out* 'And'

    17 magic] *above x'd-out* 'forms'

    18 Of] *above x'd-out* 'And'

    18 echoing] *before x'd-out* 'increases' *above which is interl. x'd-out* 'nourishes'

    18 increases] *inserted*

    19 may] *above undel.* 'doth'

   19+ [*x'd-out lines*]] 'Bearing at last a human soul as fruit, / And by gone men in ['new minds' *interl., x'd-out*] men today renew / Whence [*undel.*]'

    20 minds] 's' *interl.*

    20 out] *alt. from* 'put'

 ## #22 mutt'ring] *above x'd-out* 'feudal' *and undel.* 'priest'

    22 priests who spelled] *partly above and over* 'night ridden savage,'

    23 From . . . time] *above x'd-out* 'Wise witches'

    24 By] *after x'd-out false start* 'Fancy of poet'


## 76. *Life* (TMs)

Typewriter face 3; wove unmarked paper, 215 x 280 mm.

*Alterations:*

    6 Ashes] ('A' *in ink over* 'a'); *after del.* 'That'

    6 to] *interl. in ink w. caret*

   11 And then, a sleep] *ink-inserted w. guideline for del.* 'And [*alt. in ink from* 'At'] least,' *before undel.* 'a sleep-'

## 77. "Long time the world lay level and open" (TMs)

Typewriter face 3; laid paper marked *Treasury Linen*, chains 25 mm. apart, 188 x 215 mm., trimmed

*Emendations:*
    12 Behind] behind
    12 imprisoned] imprisioned
    14 loving] Loving

*Alterations:*
    1 lay] *in ink above del.* 'stood'
    1 level] 'le' *over* 'op'
    2 a] *in ink over illegible word*
    4 Meaningless] ('M' *in ink over* 'm', 'less' *added in ink w. caret); after del.* 'Without'
    4 thee] *after del.* 'a'
    7 ¹when] *in ink over* 'if'
    7 found,] *comma added*
    7 ²when] *in ink over* 'if'
    8 plain;] *semicolon alt. in ink from comma*
    9 Learning] *ink-inserted before del.* 'Finding'
    10 find] *in ink below ink-inserted and del.* 'make' *below del.* 'find'
    14 As] *ink-inserted*
    14 hating;] *semicolon added*
    14 it . . . go] *in ink above del.* 'that forms our weal and woe,'
    15 That] *in ink above del.* 'Thereby'
    15 creates] 'es' *in ink over* 'ing'
    15 a] *interl. in ink*
    15 from] *in ink over* 'for'
    15 things,] *comma added*
    16 Fairer . . . wings.] *above x'd-out* 'Source from which all loveliness springs.'
    18 Through . . . seen;] *under partly illegible ink revisions* 'Beyond *which [typed] [five illegible words]'
    19 is it] *in ink over* 'are they'
    20 showing] *after x'd-out* 'pass.'
    23+ [x'd-out line]] 'But, *mingling conscious [over* 'conscious, mingling'] in love's vast ocean.'
    24 swayed] *before x'd-out* 'in'
    24 mingling] *alt. from* 'mingled'
*Note:* The following trials appear after line 24:
'Conscious mingling / Rythmic ningling conscius love and reolsion. / Conscious of thw worlds tides of love / Rythmi'.

On the back of the sheet appear the lines: 'Knowing world tides of love and repulsion, / But the worlds tides of love and repulsion.'

78. *The March* (TMs)

Typewriter face 3; wove unmarked paper, 130 x 142 mm., trimmed

*Emendations:*
    2  Marched] marched
    4  New] Nw
    11 Mortals'] Mortal's
    12 griefs] grifs
    13 thoughts] thoghts
    15 plan.] ~ ∧
    16 break] brake

*Alterations:*
    8  the] *above del.* 'at'
    8  To . . . span] *above intended-del.* 'Of ineaxkyt of life'

79. "Meadows of the dawn are curtained in dusk" (TMs)

Typewriter face 3; wove unmarked paper, 179 x 246 mm., trimmed

*Emendations:*
    9  beauty] beuaty
    16 wasteful] wssteful
    16 peace] prace

*Alterations:*
    4  bootless] *above x'd-out* '[*illegible word*] other'
    5  may] *after interl. x'd-out* 'there' *above x'd-out* 'in that soil'
    6  To] *inserted before x'd-out* 'Which'
    8+ [*x'd-out words*]] 'For a future'
    9  There] *above x'd-out* 'And'
    9  save] *before partly x'd-out* 'that *wet [over* 'fed'] by tears'
    9  watered by tears] *interl. after x'd-out* 'it is wet'
    10 wonder] *after x'd-out* 'naked'
    10 naked at] *above x'd-out* 'in'
    11 women] *after x'd-out* 'lonely'
    11 possessed of] *above x'd-out* 'with'
    13 custom∧] *x'd-out comma*
    13 to wander] *after x'd-out* 'wandering'
    14 savage] *below x'd-out* 'the waste'

16  world] *before x'd-out* 'subdued is led,'
17  And] *inserted before x'd-out* 'While'
17  and] *after x'd-out* 'and'
18  Burst] ('B' *over* 'b'); *after x'd-out* 'There' *below which is x'd-out* 'the'
18  songs] *after x'd-out* 'the beauteous'
18  beauteous] *inserted*

*Note:* At the head of the page appears '2', but no first page exists.

## 80.  *The New World*— (TMs)

Typewriter face 4; wove unmarked paper, two sheets: 190 x 274 mm., 165 x 200 mm.

*Emendations:*
21  unforeseeable] unforseeable
42  loneliness] lonliness

*Alterations:*
0.1  The New World—] *added in ink*
4  distant,] *before x'd-out* 'night'
4  boundless] *interl. in ink w. caret and guideline after ink-in-interl. then del.* 'boundless'
5  As] *before x'd-out* 'filled'
5  filled] *interl. w. caret*
5  strange] *after del.* 'a'
8  a] *interl. in pencil w. caret*
11  custom,] *comma added*
14  heavens] *before x'd-out* 'and the spread out'
19  now] *in ink over* 'yet'
19  plunges] *alt. in ink from* 'plunged'
22  goes.] *in ink over* 'went.'
23  Shines] *alt. in ink from* 'shone'
23  awake] *alt. in ink from* 'awoke'
26  Each] *inserted in ink*
26  its] *in ink over* 'Their'
27  diverse,] *before x'd-out* 'and the stars nom'
28  cross.] *above x'd-out* 'cross as in'; *period added*
29  Their] ('T' *in ink over* 't'); *after del.* 'As in'
30  destiny] *after illegible word interl. in ink w. caret then del.*
30  each] *before del. illegible word*
30  alone,] *comma added*
31  silent,] *comma added*
33  Form] *in ink over* 'Make'
41  each] *after x'd-out* 'its'

44 And] *before 'where' interl. in ink w. caret then del.*
45 The] *('T' in ink); after illegible word ink-inserted then del.*

## 81. *Paradise Lost and Regained* (TMs)

Typewriter face 3; wove unmarked paper, two sheets: 181 x 270 mm., 180 x 142 mm., both trimmed

*Emendation:*
    38 When] Ehen

*Alterations:*
    4 paradise,] *comma added*
    7 fixèd] *accent added*
    9 knew∧] *x'd-out comma*
  11 beyond] *after del.* 'far'
  11 far] *interl. in ink w. caret*
  14 might] *in ink over* 'should'
  21 welcome] *after x'd-out* 'tale'
  26 And] *over* 'Anend'
  27 mingled] *before x'd-out* 'mingled'
  28 better] *moved w. caret and guideline from before* 'ever'
  30 Lovelier] *('L' in ink over* 'l'); *after del.* 'And'
  30 too] *interl. in ink w. caret*
  30 than] *before x'd-out* 'than'
  30 lovely] *after del.* 'the'
  31 man,] *comma added*
  31 good,] *comma added*
  34 With but] *interl. w. caret after interl. x'd-out* 'Who'
  34 themselves] *after x'd-out* 'That'
  34 alone] *before x'd-out* 'forever'
  34 to] *interl. w. caret*
  35 Good] *final* "s' *x'd-out*
## 35 that's] 's' *interl.; apostrophe in ink*
  37 deed] *before del.* 'done'
  37 done] *interl. in ink w. caret*
# 38 When] 'n' *in ink over* 're'

## 82. *A Peripatetic's Prayer* (TMs)

Typewriter face 1; wove unmarked paper

Two TMss exist: R: ribbon copy of first page, 170 x 250 mm.; C: carbon copy of first page, 189 x 257 mm.; T¹: ribbon copy of first draft of second page, 165 x 263 mm.; T²: ribbon copy of second draft of second page, 151 x 254 mm.; T³: carbon copy of second draft of second page, 160 x 200 mm., trimmed

Copy-text for lines 1–24 is R; for lines 25–56, T². In the list of variants, the copy-text reading appears before the bracket; unless noted as variant, T³ agrees with T².

*Variants:*

0.1 Peripatetic's] Peripatetics ('s' *added); before* 'Prayer' *in ink above del.* 'Meditation' C

14 By] *after* 'Tho' *in ink and del., over* 'But' C

24+ 2] *not present* T¹

25 [*om.*]] '¶' *ink-inserted* T¹

25 revolve;] ~, T¹

26 law,] ~ₐ T¹

28 Hard] *in ink above del.* 'Dry' *before x'd-out* 'air to' T¹

28 thin] *in ink above del.* 'moist' T¹

29 While] Black T¹

29 cold] [*rom.*] T¹, T³

30 And . . . merges] *earth from [*ink-inserted before del.* 'Water' *above del.* 'And'] water [*interl. in ink after del.* 'upon earth' *above del.* 'fixity from change'] emerges [*first 'e' added in ink*] T¹

31 [*om.*]] '¶' *ink-inserted* T¹

35 Whence] Where T¹

36 generations,] ~ₐ T¹

38 Is impotent to] *in ink above del.* 'May not nor bind nor' T¹

#39 God . . . is] far God untroubled moves not T¹

40 Who . . . solitude] *Mind that [*above x'd-out* 'Where he'] broods on Mind, highest good, [*line moved by ink guideline from below line 42*] T¹

41 Meditates . . . bliss] ['Unmoved' *del.*] By ['B' *over* 'b'] moving [*interl. in ink after x'd-out* 'eart'] world and man is sought T¹

42 Knowledge . . . good.] Eternal in Mind's solitude T¹

43 Unmoved . . . attracts] Whose unmovèd Being attracts T¹

44 —To] ₐ~ T³

44 their] the T¹

44 end,] ~ₐ T³; good, T¹

44 intelligence] Intelligence T¹

45 Things . . . wax,] The things that *changing [*moved w. guideline and caret from before* 'things'] wane and waxₐ T¹

46 For . . . essence.] Through lack of Mind's firm influence. T¹

47 [*om.*]] '¶' *ink-inserted* T¹
47 Great] Now great T¹
47 God] 'G' *over* 'g' T¹
47 gods] 'g' *over* 'G' T¹
49 world∧] ~ , T¹
49 prayer:∧] ~ :— T¹
50 By] *ink-inserted before del.* 'Through' T¹
51 last] true T¹
51 Mind] 'M' *over* 'm' T¹
52 So] Thus T¹
52 While] 'time' *in ink over* 'space' T¹
54 deed∧] ~ , T¹
55 Then . . . master] The wise master then T¹
56 while] as T¹

*Emendations:*
13 Fiercely] Firecely
26 Empyrean's] empyrean's
39 unmoved] unoved


*Alterations:*
0.1 A Peripatetic's Prayer] *inserted in ink below ink-del.* 'A Peripatetic Meditation'
8 of ] *in ink over* 'by'
11 th'] 'e' *x'd-out*
14 By] ('B' *in ink over* 'b'); *after del.* 'But'
15 cosmic] *after del.* 'the'
16 t'] 'o' *x'd-out*
17 fitful] *after x'd-out* 'fickle'
19 balloon] *after del.* 'light'
29 cold] *pencil underline*
43 h'] 'e' *x'd-out*
44 —To] *dash added in pencil;* 'To' *in pencil over* 'To'
44 end,] *comma added in pencil*
45 wane and wax] *after x'd-out* 'wax and wane'
54 city] 'ci' *over* 'th'


83. "Rough mountains once were freedom's home" (TMs)

Typewriter face 3; wove unmarked paper, two sheets: 160 x 260 mm., 180 x 133 mm.

*Emendations:*
8 freedom's] freddom's
27 best."] ~ . ∧

30 turned] turnnd
31 There] Theer

*Alterations:*

2 flags] *after pencil-del.* 'the'
2 breeze-flung] *hyphen added in pencil*
2 liberty,] *comma added in pencil*
5 mines] *after pencil-del.* 'the'
7 are] *in pencil above x'd-out* 'are the'
7 ghostly] *after pencil-del.* 'the'; *in pencil above pencil-del.* 'give saddenned'
8 sealèd] *accent added in pencil*
9 There] ('T' *in pencil over* 't'); *after pencil-del.* 'And'
14 their] *interl. in pencil w. caret*
14 who] *in pencil over* 'that'
16 work] ('ed' *x'd-out*); *before pencil-del.* 'they'
16 ceased,] *over* 'cease,'; *comma added in pencil*
18 wages;] *semicolon in pencil over period*
19 While] *in pencil above pencil-del.* 'But'
22 alive,] *comma added in pencil*
24 should] *alt. in pencil from* 'would'
26 denied;] *semicolon in pencil over illegible mark*
# 27 For . . . best."] *above x'd-out* 'Till he all other things had added since we chose the best.'
27 For] *inserted in pencil before pencil-del.* 'While'
27 them] *alt. from* 'those'
29 th'] *alt. from* 'thier'
29 Lord,] *comma added in pencil*
# 30 turned] *alt. in error from* 'turnud'; 'n' *in pencil over second* 'u'
32 on] *in pencil over* 'of'
32 wasteful] *after pencil-del.* 'flesh's'
32 lust,] *comma added in pencil*
33 And for] *inserted in pencil*
33 his] *in pencil above pencil-del.* 'And'
34 must,] *comma added in pencil*
39 and] *interl. in pencil*

84. *Sorolla* (TMs)

Typewriter face 3; laid paper marked *Treasury Linen,* chains 25 mm. apart, 168 x 215 mm.

*Emendations:*
21 tho] Tho
24 and] &

*Alterations:*

6 reserves] *final 's' in pencil over 's.'*

7 Is art:] *inserted in pencil*

9 Surface] *('S' over 's'); after x'd-out* 'Things'

9 is] *interl.*

9 not] *after x'd-out* 'should'

9 to] *interl.*

10 Tho] *inserted in pencil*

10 we] *('w' in pencil over* 'W'); *before x'd-out* 'may'

11 Solid] *final 's' del. in pencil*

11 substances] *inserted in pencil w. guideline to follow* 'Solid'

12 deckt;—] *dash added in pencil*

14 search] *in pencil above pencil-del.* 'seek'

15 show!—] *exclamation mark made in pencil from period; dash added in pencil*

16 Yet] *in pencil over* 'But'

17 stare;] *semicolon added in pencil*

18 New York] *final "s' pencil-del.*

18 a] *above x'd-out* 'the'

18 is] *added in pencil*

19 all upon the] *w. pencil guideline to replace pencil-del.* 'nought is save'

19 is] *added in pencil*

20 The] *('T' in pencil over* 't'); *after pencil-del.* 'Tis well'

20 should be] *in pencil w. guideline below pencil-del.* 'is'

# 21 E'en tho] *above x'd-out* 'E'en'

21 that are] *in pencil below x'd-out* 'that are'

22 By] *in pencil over* 'in' *above x'd-out* 'With'

# 24 With . . . lithe] *in pencil above pencil-del.* 'Bodies of men and women lithe'

*Note:* Pencil notes in right margin, most illegible and deleted, seem to be for alterations incorporated into poem.

Joaquín Sorolla y Bastida (1863–1923) was a Spanish painter noted for large landscapes in full glowing sunlight.

## 85. "Tho some of the pretty blushing ladies were shocked" (TMs)

Typewriter face 3; wove unmarked paper, 180 x 188 mm., trimmed

*Alterations:*

1 Tho] *in pencil above pencil-del.* 'And'

2 Th'] *('T' in pencil over* 't'); *after pencil-del.* 'But'

3 He] *in pencil over* 'And'

4 blossom;] *semicolon in pencil over period*
7 —Whited] *dash added in pencil*
7 starved] *interl. in pencil w. caret*
8 spirit's] *after pencil-del.* 'human'

## 86. "Through windy gorges of the clouds" (TMs)

Typewriter face 3; wove unmarked paper, 187 x 198 mm.

*Emendations:*

11 free] frue
15 lighter] lightur
16 pathway] pathsay

*Alterations:*

2 driven,] *before x'd-out* 'Sometimes lonely, more oft in crowds'
4 given.] *before x'd-out* 'Happiest they who felt the lash'
8 tracts_∧] *final period x'd-out*
9 yet] *above x'd-out* 'and'
17 But from their] *above x'd-out* 'Because of their'
20 matted] 'd' *over* 'r'
21 body's] *after x'd-out* 'unctous'

## 87. *Truth's Torch* (TMs)

Typewriter face 1; wove unmarked paper, 178 x 138 mm.

*Emendations:*

6 conceivèd] conceiveèd
7 truth's] truths'

*Alterations:*

5 lies] *alt. from* 'lied'
10 burned] 'ed' *over* 't,'
12 present] *inserted in pencil w. guideline*
12 learned.] *after pencil-del.* 'always'
13 shines] *alt. in pencil from* 'shone'
14 are] *alt. in pencil from* 'were'
16 Does] *in pencil above pencil-del.* 'would' *before pencil-del.* 'Should'
16 the] *alt. in pencil from* 'thy'
20 And] *in pencil before pencil-del.* 'To'
20 the] *alt. in pencil from* 'thy'

## 88. "Two extremes of one joinèd theme" (TMs)

Typewriter face 1; wove unmarked paper, 173 x 279 mm.

*Emendations:*
>    4 sin's] sin'
>    8 must] mus

*Alterations:*
>    7 By . . . Desire.] *above x'd-out* 'By deceiving hope of satis-
>    fied desire.'
>    14 heart's] *interl.*

## 89. *Unfaith* (TMs)

Typewriter face 1; wove unmarked paper, 139 x 207 mm.

*Emendations:*
>    10 faith's] faiths
>    11 those] whose
>    17 Were] Wre

## 90. "While world in twain allotted united was" (MS)

Lined paper, 170 x 212 mm.

*Emendations:*
>    1 allotted] alloted
>    2 ²and] &
>    3 and] &
>    6 host-grown] ~ ∧~

*Alterations:*
>    2 On] *over* 'Of'
>    2 sun's] *interl.*
>    2 land] ('d' *over* 'ds'); *before del.* 'of sun'
>    #2 mock and moan of sea] *above del.* '[*illegible word*] paths of
>    [*illegible word*]'
>    4 Thin] *above del.* 'Twas'
>    6 Speeding] *before del.* 'to'
>    #6 host-grown guests of sea] *above del.* 'guest [*illegible word*]
>    of ocean'

Note: At the bottom of the page appear the following lines with some words separated by straight lines as indicated: '['While' *del.*] the | world | in | twain | al | lot | ted | was | of land | Swam to | In twain | allotted ['of land' *del.*] | *the world | to [*interl. and moved w. caret and guideline to precede* 'In twain'] [*illegible word*] land | Swam sun and seas faithful'.

Note: In the upper right-hand corner appear the following words: 'host-grown guests of sea'.

91. "At night shining stars march in file" (TMs)

Typewriter face 3; lined paper, 169 x 210 mm., trimmed

*Emendation:*
>     4 Where] where

*Alterations:*
>     1+ [*False start*]] 'Across the' *x'd-out*
>     9 Then] *over* 'And'
>     9 next] *above x'd-out* 'the'
>     10 climbing] *after x'd-out* 'the'
>     13 And do you] *in ink above del.* 'I sometimes'
>     14 to] *in ink over* 'like'
>     16 been?] *question mark added*

92. "John Banding looked and said" (TMs)

Typewriter face 3; lined paper, three sheets: 173 x 212 mm., 172 x 211 mm., 171 x 211 mm.

*Emendations:*
>     4 pioneer.∧] ~."
>     8 see.] ~"
>     12 thee."] ~".
>     13 lone,"] ~∧"
>     16 side?∧] ~?"
>     20 might.] ~"
>     21, 45 "And] ∧~
>     32 grow?"] ~?∧
>     37 "For] ∧~
>     40 by.∧] ~."
>     49, 53 "He] ∧~

*Alterations:*
>     2 Do] *alt. in ink from* 'So'
>     4 And live as a] *in ink above del.* 'For to be a'
>     5 soil] *after x'd-out* 'lands are'
>     6 Stretchèd] *alt. in ink from* 'Stretching'
>     6 wide] *after del.* 'the'
>     8 haste there] *in ink above del.* 'that I'; *after partly-del.* 'but'
>     14 distressèd] *accent added*
>     16 stool] *before del.* 'placed'
>     16 upon] 'up' *interl. in ink*
>     #16 side?∧] *quotation mark added*
>     20 its] *in ink over* 'all'
>     25 fare] 'r' *in pencil over* 'c'

144

26 logs] *before x'd-out 'by'*
26 pilèd] *accent added in pencil*
27 may] *inserted in pencil w. guideline*
28 pierce] *in ink above del. 'come'*
30 The] *after pencil-del. 'The'*
30 sow?] *question mark alt. in pencil from comma*
46 lonely] *'n' in ink over 'v'; 'ly' over 'ely'*
46 hill] *before x'd-out 'side'*
47 their] *before undel. 'thick' ('c' in ink over 'n')*
47 thick] *interl. in ink*
50 grain;] *semicolon added*
52 wain.] *period added*
53 hard] *'h' in ink; final 's' del.*
53 trees] *alt. in ink from 'tress'*
54 their] *'ir' added*
55 sow] *before x'd-out 'and bring'*
57 "But] *(quotation mark in ink over type); over 'At'*
59 was begot] *after 'wasbe' over 'begot'*

## 93. "Next spring earth will be all in green" (TMs)

Typewriter face 1; wove paper, watermark cut off, Columbia University letterhead, 181 x 133 mm.

*Emendations:*
1 green,] green, green
10+ [om.]] When her pretty beauites will show.

*Alterations:*
#1 be all in green,] ('inb' *over* 'gr' *of undel.* 'green'); *above x'd-out* 'have a suit of'
2 her] *above x'd-out* 'its'
10 sweet] *above x'd-out* 'pretty'
10+ [om.]] *undel.* 'When ['again' *x'd-out*] her pretty beauites will show.'

## 94. #*This Child's Garden of Verse* (TMs)

Typewriter face 1; wove paper, part of watermark *agon Linen / USA*, probably Columbia University letterhead, 137 x 217 mm., trimmed; on same sheet as No. 95

*Emendation:*
0.1 Child's] Child'

*Alterations:*
    3+ [*x'd-out line*]] 'My mind in like mot'
    6 gladness] *before x'd-out* 'in her'
    6 employ;] *semicolon added*

## 95. "I should think th'earth would be ashamed" (TMs)

Typewriter face 1; wove paper, part of watermark *agon Linen /*
*USA,* probably Columbia University letterhead, 137 x 217 mm.,
trimmed; on same sheet as No. 94

*Emendation:*
    3 so,] ~.

## 97. "Like formless fog on aimless cruise" (MS)

*Emendation:*
    6 gleam] gleame

*Alterations:*
    1 aimless] 'ess' *over illegible letters*
    5 may] *over* 'can' *over* 'do'
  #6 gleam] 'gl' *over* 'be'
    7 Now] *over* 'Then'
    8 blue in peace] *above del.* 'peace now'
    9 o'erspanned] 'o'er' *over* 'over'

## 98. *To a Pedant* (TMs)

*Emendations:*
    19 second-handed] ~ ∧ ~
    19 auctions] acutions
    27 catch] cathch
    28 Any] And
    29 unbidden] undidden

*Alterations:*
    0.1 [*undel. title*]] To a [*over illegible letter*] Peadnt ['P' *over* 'p']
    3 and] ('d' *over* 'f'); *before undel.* 'fu' ['u' *over* 'l']
    3 garnisht∧] ('g' *over* 'l'); *comma x'd-out*
    5 hall] 'h' *over* 'f'
    9 some] *above x'd-out* 'a'
    15 four] *after partly x'd-out* 'some'
    18 engraven] 'en' *added*

19  bought] 'b' *over* 's'
25  pompous] *before* x'd-out 'specimen'
30  To] *before del.* 'disturb'
30  dim] *inserted and encircled in ink*

# Index of Titles

|  | PAGE NUMBER |
|---|---|
| Across the white of my mind's map, 25 | 18 |
| *America*, 63 | 47 |
| And high God on his throne, 64 | 47 |
| And shall we shut the door, 65 | 48 |
| And the lad eager replied: No sir, not a God damned Word, 66 | 48 |
| At night shining stars march in file, 91 | 71 |
| *At the Last*, 26 | 18 |
| Athwart the shining gleam, 96 | 77 |
| *Autumn*, 1 | 3 |
|  |  |
| Because the plan of world is dim and blurred, 67 | 49 |
| *Blossoming Wilderness, The*, 2 | 3 |
| *Borrowed*, 68 | 49 |
| *Brave Things*, 69 | 50 |
| *But*, 70 | 50 |
|  |  |
| *Child's Garden, The*, 27 | 19 |
| *Creation*, 47 | 35 |
|  |  |
| Dear moon and stars, and dearer yet, 48 | 36 |
| *Duplicity*, 71 | 51 |
|  |  |
| Earth-born dust rising in the air, 49 | 37 |
| *Education*, 72 | 51 |
| Empty as high heaven's heartless shell, 3 | 4 |
|  |  |
| Fair flowers grow in my garden ground, 50 | 37 |
| *Fallow Field, A*, 51 | 38 |
| *Forgetfulness*, 73 | 53 |
| From my glance backward sent recedes, 52 | 38 |
|  |  |
| Generations of stifled worlds reaching out, 4 | 4 |
|  |  |
| He failed. Though he was strong, 28 | 19 |
| Heaven and ground, smooth sky and shore, 74 | 54 |
| *Hope and Memory*, 5 | 5 |

148

I should think th'earth would be ashamed, 95    74
I wake from the long, long night, 6    5
*In Light*, 7    6
*In the Country*, 53    39
*Indian Summer at the Farm*, 54    39
Is this the end, 8    6

John Banding looked and said, 92    71
*Journey, A*, 55    40

Language, fourth dimension of the mind, 75    54
Last night I stood upon the hill, 29    20
*Life*, 76    55
Life blithe in lusty action restless and rude, 56    40
Like fogs from some black cave of mournful night, 57    41
Like formless fog on aimless cruise, 97    77
*Little Things*, 30    20
Long time lay the world level and open, 31    21
Long time the world lay level and open, 77    56

*March, The*, 78    56
Meadows of the dawn are curtained in dusk, 79    57
*Mine Own Body*, 32    22
*Moment and a Time, A*, 58    41
*Mountain's Hour, The*, 59    42
*My Body and My Soul*, 9    7
*My Fever*, 33    23
My mind is but a gutt'ring candle dip, 34    23
*My Road*, 35    24

*Natural Magic*, 10    8
*New World, The*, 80    58
Next spring earth will be all in green, 93    73
Not now thy scourging rod, 36    24
Not wrinkled, shrivelled, grey, 37    24
Now night, mother soul, broods the weary hours, 60    42

*One Night*, 11    9

*Paradise Lost and Regained*, 81    59
*Peripatetic's Prayer, A*, 82    60
*Postponement*, 12    9
*Pulse in an Earthen Jar*, 38    25

*Renewal*, 61    43
*Respite*, 39    26

| | |
|---|---:|
| *Romance,* 40 | 26 |
| Rope is cut, the anchor falls, The, 62 | 43 |
| Rough mountains once were freedom's home, 83 | 62 |
| *Round of Passion, The,* 13 | 9 |
| | |
| *Song,* 14 | 10 |
| *Sorolla,* 84 | 63 |
| *Swinburnian,* 15 | 10 |
| | |
| That frail ship I load with limitless freight, 41 | 27 |
| There stirred within me, 16 | 11 |
| *This Child's Garden of Verse,* 94 | 73 |
| Tho all the rhymes were long since rhymed, 42 | 28 |
| Tho some of the pretty blushing ladies were shocked, 85 | 63 |
| *Thoughts,* 17 | 12 |
| Through windy gorges of the clouds, 86 | 64 |
| *Thy Mind,* 18 | 13 |
| *Ties,* 19 | 13 |
| *Time Laid Low,* 20 | 14 |
| *To a Pedant,* 98 | 78 |
| *To Conscience,* 43 | 28 |
| *To Death,* 44 | 29 |
| To us you came from out of dark, 45 | 30 |
| *Truth's Torch,* 87 | 64 |
| *Two Births,* 46 | 30 |
| Two extremes of one joinèd theme, 88 | 65 |
| *Two Joys,* 21 | 14 |
| *Two Weeks,* 22 | 14 |
| | |
| *Unending Hours, The,* 23 | 17 |
| *Unfaith,* 89 | 66 |
| | |
| *When Thou Art Gone,* 24 | 18 |
| While world in twain allotted united was, 90 | 67 |

# Index of First Lines

POEM
NUMBER

A pool of clear waters thy mind                                          18
A wail, a cry                                                            76
About the earth whereon we dwell                                        70
Across the white of my mind's map                                      25
Adown the mottled slopes of night                                      35
And high God on his throne                                             64
And shall we shut the door                                             65
And the lad eager replied: No sir, not a God damned Word              66
And this is art                                                         84
"Arouse! Fight on! Combat and conquer                                 43
Art thou there, my love                                                44
At night shining stars march in file                                  91
Athwart the shining gleam                                              96

Because the plan of world is dim and blurred                          67

Close by the clouds' quick built up ledge                             58
Could we peep within thy mind                                         98

Dear moon and stars, and dearer yet                                   48
Deep shadowed in the dim remoteness of night's high tower             59

Earth-born dust rising in the air                                     49
Empty as high heaven's heartless shell                                 3
E'en in joy remember, Sweet                                           21

Fair flowers grow in my garden ground                                 50
Fair is my love in body's grace                                        1
Fog flowers uncurled at morn                                          54
For I who am a feeble thing                                           30
From my glance backward sent recedes                                  52

Generations of stifled worlds reaching out                            4
Glad at birth, nestled on earth                                       17
God walked the earth                                                  11

He failed. Though he was strong                          28
He tiptoed springily, standing still                     40
Heaven and ground, smooth sky and shore                  74
Heaven's one star                                         7

I dreamed a languid dream of soft deceit                  2
I hardly think I heard you call                          72
I lie upon the ground                                    23
I should think th'earth would be ashamed                 95
I wake from the long, long night                          6
In arid spaces as yet unsown of sun                      47
Is this the end                                           8
It's streaked with grime                                 38

John Banding looked and said                             92

Language, fourth dimension of the mind                   75
Last night I stood upon the hill                         29
Life blithe in lusty action restless and rude            56
Like fogs from some black cave of mournful night         57
Like formless fog on aimless cruise                      97
Like the moving sea's wide liberty                       10
Like the voyaging of the dim uncertainties               53
Long time lay the world level and open                   31
Long time the world lay level and open                   77
Love's light tether                                      19

Meadows of the dawn are curtained in dusk                79
Musing on memories of things that were                   73
My body of crowding pains a vase                         33
My heart was all unready                                 12
My mind is but a gutt'ring candle dip                    34

Next spring earth will be all in green                   93
Not for the sun to say                                   68
Not now thy scourging rod                                36
Not wrinkled, shrivelled, grey                           37
Now hearken and I'll relate the wile                     81
Now night, mother soul, broods the weary hours           60

Of a sudden, a blazing star                              80
Of fraud and force fast woven                            78
Old earth shows new with growing grass                   14
Or ere I sought the golden fleece                        46

Riches, possessions hold me? Nay                                      22
Rough mountains once were freedom's home                              83

Silent I sat in the darkness                                          61
Since far spaces cannot part                                          94
Swift moving earth that gallant hung                                  69

That frail ship I load with limitless freight                        41
Th'Empyrean ever whirls                                              82
The meaning of these things I've read in books I do not know          9
The rope is cut, the anchor falls                                    62
The shallow seas o'errun the sand                                    39
There in the surf of that sulphurous sea                             15
There stirred within me                                              16
Think not the torch                                                  87
Tho all the rhymes were long since rhymed                            42
Tho half my heart might keep on singing                               5
Tho some of the pretty blushing ladies were shocked                  85
Thou opened wide thy gates                                           63
Through slow dull years                                              13
Through windy gorges of the clouds                                   86
Thy mem'ry drives the restless brook                                 24
Time with his old flail                                              20
To us you came from out of dark                                      45
Tumult and peace I strove to share                                   32
Two extremes of one joinèd theme                                     88
Two men arose to teach the race                                      71

Virgin waters and veilèd snows                                       55

Waving weeds of sprightly ladies                                     51
While world in twain allotted united was                             90
With you who do not now believe                                      89
Would God my feet might lead                                         27

Ye mete me now your measures                                         26